ADULTING LIFE SKILLS FOR YOUNG ADULTS: BEYOND THE BASICS

NAVIGATE THROUGH HIGH SCHOOL, COLLEGE, AND INTO THE WORLD WITH INNER KNOWLEDGE AND THE ABILITY TO THRIVE INDEPENDENTLY

JAQUI MEYER

© **Copyright 2023 Jaqui Meyer - All rights reserved.**

The content contained within this book may not be reproduced, duplicated or transmitted without direct written permission from the author or the publisher.

Under no circumstances will any blame or legal responsibility be held against the publisher, or author, for any damages, reparation, or monetary loss due to the information contained within this book, either directly or indirectly.

Legal Notice:

This book is copyright protected. It is only for personal use. You cannot amend, distribute, sell, use, quote or paraphrase any part, or the content within this book, without the consent of the author or publisher.

Disclaimer Notice:

Please note the information contained within this document is for educational and entertainment purposes only. All effort has been executed to present accurate, up to date, reliable, complete information. No warranties of any kind are declared or implied. Readers acknowledge that the author is not engaged in the rendering of legal, financial, medical or professional advice. The content within this book has been derived from various sources. Please consult a licensed professional before attempting any techniques outlined in this book.

By reading this document, the reader agrees that under no circumstances is the author responsible for any losses, direct or indirect, that are incurred as a result of the use of the information contained within this document, including, but not limited to, errors, omissions, or inaccuracies.

CONTENTS

Introduction	5
1. FIND OUT WHO YOU ARE	9
Values, Ethics, Morals, Principles, and Beliefs: What's the Difference?	10
Defining Your Core Values and Personal Beliefs	13
Self-Love	22
Stop Feeling Unworthy	26
The Power of Affirmations	35
Key Takeaways	37
2. DEVELOP AND USE YOUR THINKING SKILLS	39
Why Creative Thinking Is Essential	40
Flexible Thinking	46
Critical Thinking	49
Key Takeaways	52
3. INDEPENDENCE DAY	55
Get Educated	57
On the Job	58
Goals	66
Time Management	72
Healthy Habits	75
Let's Get Practical	80
Key Takeaways	88
4. DOLLARS AND SENSE	93
Money Management Tips	94
Key Takeaways	100
5. LET'S GET PERSONAL	101
Family and Friends	102
Romantic Relationships	116
Effective Communication	127
Key Takeaways	131

6. FACING THE HARD STUFF	133
Substance Abuse and Addiction	133
Mental Health	138
Key Takeaways	140
Conclusion	143
References	147

INTRODUCTION

Adulting is hard—take it from someone who's had to do it for over 40 years already. The world is a crazy place riddled with chaos and confusion, and if you don't have the skills to navigate these unsafe waters, you're surely going to drown. I have to admit, you have it much worse than I did. Growing up was simpler back then.

"I was your age once, you know," is something that I often say to my children but, in reality, that statement is limited to simple anatomy—nothing more. Violence is spiraling out of control, and the political atmosphere is thick with dissension, more so than ever before. Social media brings with it a whole new level of trouble. Previous generations didn't have to worry that their not-so-wise choices would end up on the internet for the world to see, forever; you do. You have the added social pressure and risk that stems from social media to deal with. The constant worry about what you're doing, saying, how you look, or with whom you're hanging out is beyond tiring, but if you don't do it, all it takes is a tweet, photo, or video, and your life is ruined. Cyberbullying is a reality I didn't ever have to deal with.

There's a constant spotlight on you, and the amount of responsibility that comes with that sucks away your innocence at an alarming rate. You are part of a generation of youth in crisis, and the world is not prepared for it; but, luckily, you can prepare for it. To grow up into a competent and well-adjusted adult, you will need to work a little harder than I or your parents had to, and I'm here to help you. It is my job to guide you; to be your compass. I don't want your young adult life to get off to a rocky start. I never want you to have to use the words "low-paying job," "bad credit," or "unhealthy relationships" when talking about your life.

With some basic life skills and guidance, it will be easier for you to figure out where you're heading, and how to get there in one piece. It's not a walk in the park transitioning into adulthood, especially since it's that time in our lives when we think we know everything. I can tell you now, you may know some of what you need to know, but you don't know it all.

As a mother, grandmother, and great-grandmother, all of whom have unique quirks and personalities, I knew I had to write this book to help young adults.

Young adults are inundated with hard choices, varying values and beliefs, and principles. You have to get to know yourself to make choices that are authentic to your goals. The tools in this book will be a huge helping hand as you venture into the world.

1

FIND OUT WHO YOU ARE

One of the most important things you can do to make sure that you'll live a happy and fulfilled life is to get to know yourself. If you don't know who you are, you won't know what you want in life, and that means making your dreams come true won't be possible.

Living an inauthentic life is extremely frustrating, and worse yet, it is such a waste. YOLO, right? So, to make the best out of the one chance you have, you need to discover who you are at the core. Considering the fact that people change, learning about yourself is a never-ending task, but don't let that discourage you. Self-discovery can be exciting. Think about it, the more you know about yourself, the closer you'll get to living a life that is tailored to your needs and wants. You'll wake up each morning with a smile because you'll be excited about what lies ahead. The alternative is a life where you hate the job you have, dislike the house you live in, are caught in a marriage with someone whom you don't really like—the list goes on and on.

When you jump on the internet and do a quick search on "how to get to know yourself," words like "values," "beliefs," "ethics," and more are often used. Things quickly become confusing as these terms are so close in meaning and often overlap. This makes answering the question, "Who am I?" challenging.

In this chapter, we're going to look at the meanings of these words and where they fit in on your road to self-discovery. I'll also help you with tools to establish your core values. This is important because your core values guide you; they help you navigate the meandering roads of life. Think of your core values as a moral compass—they dictate your behavior and help you distinguish between right and wrong.

Living a life true to you just hits differently; so let's get to work.

VALUES, ETHICS, MORALS, PRINCIPLES, AND BELIEFS: WHAT'S THE DIFFERENCE?

It's difficult to distinguish between these terms as they often are used interchangeably to describe what makes a person *good*. However, if you have clarity on the true meaning of values, principles, beliefs, ethics, and morals, then you'll be able to better define yours, which means you'll become more aware of who you are.

I care about the influences of today's world and how they affect you. Getting through high school and getting ready to go out into the world isn't easy. I wish I had been given this information when I was younger.

In this book, I'm going to share with you everything I wish I knew while growing up, but the words written here aren't only based on my experience (or lack thereof, rather) as a young adult. It also contains all the knowledge I gained from raising my kids and seeing them struggle with transitioning from being taken care of to caring for themselves.

After reading *Adulting Life Skills for Young Adults: Beyond the Basics*, I want you to say, "I got this!" If you apply the things you read in this book, you'll be more equipped than others to overcome the challenges you'll face as you venture out into the world. What's more, you can take the skills you'll learn here and apply them throughout your whole life. We'll cover topics like money management, goal-setting skills, healthy habits, relationships, career guidance, further education, self-care and self-love, mental health, and much more! These are recurring themes in your life, so if you can build a strong foundation now, your future will be less complicated.

I think it is time we start, don't you? You may be a noob at this young adult thing, but once you put this book down, you'll have all the knowledge you need to reach the level of an expert.

Ethics and Morals

You've probably heard about ethics and morals, and it is likely that you believe they have the same meaning; you wouldn't be entirely wrong. The main difference between these two terms is the level of internalization. Ethics recommends what is right and wrong on a group level, whereas morals are the personal acceptance of ethics (Internet Encyclopaedia of Philosophy, n.d.).

In other words, you may follow the ethics of a specific group—school, church, workplace, family—but if you haven't taken on their standards at a personal level, then you don't have the morals of that particular group. It's also possible for you to violate the ethics of a group because they don't align with your personal moral standards.

It's a small difference and some may even say we're being pedantic by distinguishing between ethics and morals, but it is important that we do. Why? You need to know if you agree with what society expects of you or whether you have a different idea of how you should live your life. That is a big step toward living an authentic life.

Principles and Values

Although both principles and values deal with a person's moral position, there's a difference in how set they are. Principles are objective and universal—they're not affected by cultures or individuals. Values, on the other hand, are more fluid; they're internal and subjective. Let's look at Starbucks as an example.

The management of the company may have honesty as a principle because that is just what is expected; it is universally correct. But they can also have trendiness and hipness as values to secure their place in the industry.

The values of trendiness and hipness are justified by the value they add to the business. If Starbucks wants to change its focus to washing cars, as a wild example, "trendy" and "hip" won't necessarily serve the purpose of the company any longer, while the principle of honesty still does.

Often, ethical codes are built on principles. If the ethical standards of an organization don't align with accepted principles, there will be pushback in the future. For example, gender equality is a global principle and if it isn't included in the ethical standards of a university, business, or any other establishment, it won't be long before people become unhappy.

Virtues and Beliefs

Virtue covers ethics and morals. Think of it as an evaluation of your morals as defined by others. For example, some communities classify hard work as a virtue, while in others, chastity is. You also get virtues that are established by religion, organizations, or other bodies that hold a position of power. You can sum up virtues as a person's attitude, disposition, and character that help them act according to established principles (Velasquez et al., n.d.).

Then there are beliefs: The internalization of ethics and principles, which get transformed into morals and virtues. Beliefs are what make it possible for us to express the good within ourselves.

What Does This All Mean?

Not everyone finds debating the philosophical meaning of words exciting, but in this case, it is important to know as it can help you make sense of what the world expects of you—or better yet, what you expect of yourself. Comprehending the subtle differences between these ideologies ultimately helps you understand human behavior. It will make it easier for you to explain why a friend of yours is angry about the university's code of conduct and will give you the information you need to discover if you want to be angry too. That's only one example of many. Furthermore, if you plan on stepping into a leadership role, being able to differentiate between morals, virtues, and beliefs will take you a long way, as these areas can help you drive change in your organization when needed.

The bottom line is that these aren't just words to throw around interchangeably; each one has its own meaning and with that, its own significance and consequence. Focusing on the true meaning of each will benefit you as you go through life.

DEFINING YOUR CORE VALUES AND PERSONAL BELIEFS

So far, we've established that living a fulfilling life is only possible when you live an authentic life. This is where your core values and personal beliefs come in—your happiness will be built on these. When you have these beliefs and values clearly defined, it's as if the fog clears up and the road ahead of you is clear again. The world is ever-changing but when you know what you believe in, you'll stay grounded while everyone is shifting around you. That is because core values are unchangeable; they're not affected by the media, your social circle, or anything else. They're rooted in you, right down into your core.

The first step, however, is to outline exactly what your core beliefs and personal values are before you can experience the comforting effect of knowing what you stand for.

To start, we have to look at personal values. In other words, we need to examine what behavior and qualities guide you in your decision-making and actions. Personal values are as the name suggests, personal. They differ from person to person and are shaped by where and how you grow up and your life experiences.

Honesty and kindness are only two examples of personal values, but there are unlimited possibilities. When you're guided by your values, you're likely to live a better and more fulfilled life. On the flip side, if you don't live according to your values, you may end up feeling bad about yourself, and you may ques-tion your reason for living or your purpose.

Personal values have a profound effect on your life right down to the small day-to-day decisions you make, not to mention the life-altering choices you have to make. This is why it is vitally important for you to know what your values are. One way to do this is to create a value statement.

Businesses usually create value statements as a way to guide their way forward, but it can work just as well in a personal sense.

Unsure what a value statement is? Basically, it is a summary of what is important to you, what you want to prioritize in your life, and how you will behave to reach your goals. For example, if you value living a simple life, you'll feel stressed and anxious when you're pressured to live a pretentious life. However, if you value living ostentatiously, the reverse is true; an unassuming and modest life will leave you feeling disappointed and craving more.

As mentioned, personal values are limitless and there's no universal list you can go through to pick your values from. Yet, according to Schwarts (1992), there are ten categories each value will fit into:

1. Achievement: Success, determination, accomplishment…
2. Benevolence: Loyal, forgiving, supportive, responsible…
3. Conformity: Respect, restraint, politeness…
4. Hedonism: Pleasure, indulgence…
5. Power: Wealth, authority…
6. Security: Social order…
7. Self-direction: Originality, freedom…
8. Stimulation: Daring, excitement…
9. Tradition: Modest, devout, respectful of tradition…
10. Universalism: Equality, social justice, wisdom, protecting the environment…

Now that you know more about core values, let's look at core beliefs and how they affect your life.

Let's start with defining what core beliefs are. They can be described as the fundamental ideas and opinions you have about yourself, the world, and the future. These beliefs aren't absolute but are necessary to understand humankind. Beliefs are usually established during childhood and during other formative stages of your life.

Examples of sources of beliefs are:

- **Association:** When you interact with others.
- **Authority:** Influential people in your life, such as your parents, pastor or other religious leader, and school teacher, can help you develop your beliefs.
- **Evidence:** Your own experiences and what you learned from them can synthesize your beliefs.
- **Tradition:** Your family and community traditions play a role in developing your beliefs.

Your beliefs also fall into categories of self, others, the world, and the future, as well as being labeled as either positive (enabling) or negative (limiting).

Enabling Beliefs

When your beliefs are positive and portray optimism and trust in yourself and your abilities, then they are classified as enabling beliefs.

Some examples of positive beliefs include:

- Life is good.
- I'm competent.
- I always give my best.
- People are kind.
- I am hardworking.
- My future is looking upbeat.

Limiting Beliefs

Negative beliefs, on the other hand, are characterized as unconstructive and damaging. These beliefs hold you back from reaching your full potential, and although these beliefs are inaccurate and unhelpful, they're seen as absolutes. People who have limiting beliefs are usually extremely judgmental of themselves and others.

Examples of negative beliefs include:

- My life has no meaning.
- I'm useless.
- I never give my all.
- People are mean-spirited.
- I'm lazy.
- My future is looking dreadful.

You also have to know that beliefs—positive and negative—aren't always accurate. In fact, they can at times be so wrong that they can lead you to make bad decisions. On the flip side, enabling beliefs, even when inaccurate, can lead to decisions that end up making your life better. It's confusing, I know, but if you get the hang of this self-discovery business, you'll be able to figure out whether your beliefs will lead to a good place or not.

We've established that getting to know yourself is at the center of winning at life. If you're not sure where to start on your journey of self-exploration, below are some questions you can ask yourself to get underway. Write down the answers as they come to mind, otherwise, they're not going to be truthful enough to give you the insights you need to identify your core values and beliefs.

Who do you admire?

Identifying real-life people who you look up to can give you a unique perspective into yourself. Consider the people you admire and have a high regard for. It can be a friend or family member, celebrity, or even a character in one of your favorite books or movies. Once you have someone in mind, get more specific; ask yourself what about them inspires you, what commendable qualities they have, and which of their actions or manners you want to mimic.

You can take it further by looking at all the qualities they possess and identifying what you need to work on to become more like them.

What moves you to action?

For the most part, your actions and behaviors are driven by your core values and beliefs. Think back to a situation where you stood up for someone or something. What pushed you to take action?

Write down the feelings that drove you to speak up or act. What risks did you take or were you willing to take at that moment? Finally, what were the consequences of your actions? In other words, did you gain or lose something?

When do you feel your most authentic?

The times in your life when you feel most like yourself, are the times when you're closest to living your values and beliefs. The times when you go against your core, you may feel shame or guilt.

Think of times when things just felt wrong and you had to face shame or guilt. Who were you with, what exact feelings did you experience, and what were the emotional and physical results?

Next, think of situations where you felt authentic and your actions and behaviors were genuine. Again, answer the following questions:

- Who were you with?
- What exact feelings did you experience?
- What were the emotional and physical results?

The two sets of answers above give great insight into your values and beliefs. Study them, and in the future, try to stick to situations where you don't have to be someone you're not.

Live Your Core Values

It's about more than just knowing what your core values and beliefs are; you have to live them! If you want to see a difference in your life, your values need to go from written words to practical actions. Sounds easy enough, right? Unfortunately, living authentically is one of the more challenging things to get right. You're bombarded with images of how you *should* live, what you *should* do, and what is good social behavior, and what isn't. That makes it challenging to live your life as you want without the fear of being outcast for going against the grain.

It takes a lot of courage to live life on your own terms. To help it become second nature, here are two simple ways to apply your values and beliefs to your daily life.

Use It to Set Goals

Setting goals is paramount if you want to live a life worth living. You have to live with purpose; otherwise, what's the point? You've already been setting small goals; you just don't realize it. Acing an exam, finishing high school, starting college, leaving home, those are all goals—they're part of growing up. Of course, that doesn't mean you won't set goals as you get older. Nope. You'll continue to have aspirations: buying a car or a new home, getting married, finding your dream job, and climbing the ladder until you're at the top of the corporate food chain. Whatever your goals are, think of your core values and beliefs when you set them. Don't let your life deviate from them or you won't be too happy with the person staring back at you in the mirror and the way their life has turned out.

Use It to Guide Your Decisions

Your values and beliefs shouldn't just be applied to major life decisions. They should guide your day-to-day choices as well. When faced with decisions throughout your day, how do you react? Better yet, does your reaction correspond with your values? Let me give you an example. If you see compassion as one of your core values, do you treat people with kindness or are you actually judgmental and critical of others?

There will be times when your behavior won't align with your values—it's hard to let go of old habits and it's easy to lose sight of what you expect of yourself, so you end up responding in a way you don't want to.

To help you be more conscious about your values and beliefs and the role they should play in your daily life, you can do the following:

- Keep your list of core values and beliefs next to your bed and make a point of reading them aloud each morning.
- Before you get out of bed, visualize the day ahead. Imagine how you will live up to your values throughout the day.
- Make a copy of your list of core values and beliefs and carry it with you for when you need guidance to make a decision.
- Set your values and beliefs as backgrounds on your phone and laptop. This will be a constant reminder of how to behave.

- Use your phone or calendar to set reminders of your values and beliefs throughout the day.

At times, when you realize you strayed from your values and beliefs, take time to analyze what happened and ask yourself what you could've done differently.

SELF-LOVE

"Love makes the world go round." If you haven't heard that saying before, it's only a matter of time before you do. But I would like to change things up a little and replace "love" with "self-love." The power loving yourself has over the course of your life is not taken seriously enough. There's a big focus on finding your soulmate, the person you want to grow old with and give your all to. If you ask me, the passion, self-acceptance, and devotion you have for yourself is the most special love story of your life.

I realize the concept of self-love may be a foreign concept for your young adult brain, but for now, all you need to accept is that it is the cornerstone of your happiness. All other aspects of the "self" are built on top of it: awareness, compassion, esteem, respect, expression, and so on. Self-love is a fundamental part of connecting with yourself in the most genuine way.

Let's explore the concept of self-love a little closer by defining what it means. The most basic definition of *self-love* is the ability to fully appreciate yourself on a mental, physical, and spiritual level. As a result, you'll feel worthy to occupy space in this world, experience peace, and above all, be happy.

There's one big obstacle on your road to self-love: social media. Spending too much time browsing what influencers, celebrities, and models are up to is a surefire way to drop your mood and self-esteem. When these "perfect" lives are flaunted in front of you constantly, you won't be able to stop yourself from comparing your circumstances to theirs, and of course, you're going to fall short. You know what? Most people will fall short because what they see on social media isn't real; it doesn't exist. You only get to see what they want you to see and, on top of that, through various filters. Their struggles aren't shared openly, so it is very easy to forget that they have any at all.

I'm not going to ask you to stay off of social media. I am, however, going to teach you some techniques you can use to start taking care of yourself. Don't neglect this part of the process of growth; self-love has many benefits, including the ability to bounce back quickly from trying times and being more emotionally resilient.

If you do feel that self-love is a waste of time, you may want to reconsider your position as having low self-esteem, which, when linked to a lack of self-care, actually shrinks your brain (Ghosh, n.d.). This affects your memory, emotions, and control of movement. I suggest a "better safe than sorry" approach—it's not like anyone is asking you to do something horrible.

How to Practice Self-Love

My daughter had a journal full of Rumi quotes and she'd share one with me every Sunday night before going to bed. One night, she read to me one of his most famous quotes: "Your task is not to seek for love, but merely to seek and find all the barriers within yourself that you have built against it."

As with all of his sayings, I couldn't help but think about what he meant. The first thing that came to mind was that he was saying love is all around us; all we need to do is break down the walls within that are preventing us from seeing it. That, on its own, is already a valuable lesson, but what if he also meant to say that, we don't need to look for love on the outside, but instead, break down all the barriers inside us that are stopping us from loving ourselves?

The fact of the matter is that self-love is natural, but society conditions us to look for all the areas where we're "not enough" —not smart enough, successful enough, skinny enough, rich enough, and so on. Every time you believe you fall short of what society deems ideal, you're placing a brick in the wall that is stopping you from loving yourself, and before you know it, you won't be able to see any reason why you deserve to be loved by anyone.

So, how do you rise above the noise?

1. Be Careful What You Say to Yourself

Each of us has an inner bully. They're not very nice and will try to break you down every chance they get. You have to learn to quiet this critical inner voice. The first step to getting it under control is to become extra aware of how you talk to yourself. You need to pay attention to what you say to yourself in your mind and how it makes you feel. Do you constantly tell yourself that you're useless, worthless, that nobody loves you, or worse? These are the thoughts you have to push aside if you want to practice self-love. You need to tell that bully, "Stop it. I'm not what you say I am. I am kind, I'm driven, I'm passionate…" You need to respond with a positive fact about yourself if you want to take away your inner critic's power. Later on, we'll look at the power of affirmations. This daily practice is an excellent way to disprove all the negative things you tell yourself.

2. Clear Your Mind

It's difficult to see the beautiful view outside if the window is fogged up. Similarly, you won't be able to see your true self and your dreams if your mind is clouded by societal beliefs, and other people's beliefs and values. You need to make sure you can see your values and beliefs clearly if you want to live an authentic life—the ultimate form of self-love.

3. Take Care of Yourself

You can't just practice self-care once a week; you need to love yourself daily. Eating a healthy diet, exercising, making sure that you get a good night's sleep, and socializing with friends and family are self-love habits you should stick to each day. When you take care of your body, you take care of your mind. For example, if you wake up refreshed, it is much more likely that you'll be in a good mood, which will boost your confidence levels. When you feel good about yourself, you'll say "Yes" to doing more things that you love and this will give you an endorphin boost big enough to make the smile on your face last well into the day.

4. Believe in Boundaries

"No" is not a curse word. I want you to acknowledge this so that you can move on to live a life with boundaries. When you don't have boundaries, you're more likely to agree to do things that steal your joy and lead to unhappiness. Let's take your career, for example. If you don't have limits, nothing is stopping your boss and coworkers from abusing you. Working late, having to be available 24/7, and being overloaded with work usually happens when someone doesn't stand up for themselves, and doesn't make clear what they will and will not accept. Allowing yourself to be treated like a doormat is not self-love.

STOP FEELING UNWORTHY

It's not a pleasant feeling when you feel you can't do anything right or question if you're worthy of all the good that happens in your life. Don't worry, you're not alone; many people experience feelings of unworthiness at some point in time.

A lack of self-confidence is one of the key driving forces behind feeling like you're not good enough. As you go through life, there are many experiences that will leave you questioning your value. You may even come across people who tell you you're insignificant. As your self-confidence diminishes due to these incidents, it becomes even more challenging to shake feelings of unworthiness.

The best way to guard against outside circumstances affecting your self-confidence is to understand why it happens in the first place.

People Tell You That You're Not Good Enough

I often wonder why some people have the need to put others down. Is it because they grew up in a household where they were told they were not good enough, not worthy, or useless? That's very likely.

Whatever the reason may be for their behavior, caring about what others think is an inborn trait, which makes it very difficult to ignore these slights (Hendriksen, 2016). The reason why we care goes back to our ancestors; being liked was the difference between life and death. If we weren't accepted by the group, we were banished and left out in the cold, without shelter, or food. Yes, we're not living in those circumstances anymore, but social acceptance is still entrenched in our existence.

You Tell Yourself That You're Not Good Enough

This circles back to the previous section where we discussed your inner bully. If you grew up in circumstances where you were constantly hearing negative things about yourself, it is going to be extra hard to get rid of negative self-talk. The voices of the people who attack you will echo in your mind. What you need to do is remind yourself that the thoughts you're having aren't your own.

As you become more aware of the way you talk to yourself, you need to stop and ask why you're telling yourself you're not good enough. Is it because you're copying what someone else said? Take the time to figure out where these thoughts are coming from.

Whenever I saw my children struggle with negative self-talk, I would remind them that they wouldn't say that to a friend, so why aren't they being friends with themselves?

You're Not Resilient Enough

You have to *want* to create a life worth living. It's only then that you'll have the resilience to stand up when life knocks you down. All of us feel down at some point in time, but this state of mind is easy to overcome if you're mentally strong enough.

You have to work on being more resilient if you want to feel better about yourself. The good news is that if you're more resilient, you'll be more self-confident, which will boost your resilience. This is a self-improvement cycle you want to be stuck in! Since *Adulting Life Skills for Young Adults* is all about moving toward your goals, self-discovery, self-love, maintaining a positive outlook, and self-care—all aspects that build resilience—you're on the right path to becoming hardier.

Here are four activities and exercises you can do to build resilience:

Breathe. Breathing is a great way to modulate your emotions. There are different exercises you can do depending on what works for you.

Some people find that if they sit and count to five as they breathe in and to seven on an exhale, they calm down significantly. Others shift their focus from negative emotions by placing one hand on their chest and the other on their abdomen. As they breathe, they concentrate on how their body is moving.

The most basic way you can use breathing to regulate your emotions is as easy as sitting back, closing your eyes, and taking a few deep breaths until you can feel your mind quiet down and the stress and negativity melt away.

Let go. Our inability to release emotions is often a contributing factor to the dysregulation we experience. Even if you're self-aware enough to realize your thoughts are irrational, and so too are the emotions that flow from them, you may still find it challenging to eliminate them from your mind.

When you undergo an emotional purging, you can achieve the mental balance that comes with letting go.

Here are the steps you should follow to release unwanted emotions:

- Observe your emotions. Don't attempt to change them but allow them to take up space.
- Examine the physical experiences your emotions trigger.
- Recognize that although your feelings are part of you, they're not you. Your emotions come and go; for example, you may feel sad, but that doesn't mean you suffer from depression.

- Name the emotions and write them down.
- Talk about them. You can confide in a friend, or family member, or speak to a therapist to help you objectively release negative emotions.

Learn to live in the present. A big part of mindfulness is living in the moment. The more you practice mindfulness, the easier it will be to become aware of your mind, body, and feelings. With this skill, you'll be able to approach your emotions from a neutral perspective. It gives you the ability to take the emotion, out of the emotion, and deal with it objectively.

Become self-aware. Self-awareness is such a powerful skill. It goes hand in hand with mindfulness and is another way for you to recognize your emotions and how they make you feel. To manage your emotions, you have to do some investigating. Start by making a list of all the thoughts that are running through your mind at the moment. What is causing these thoughts? Name the people or explain the circumstances you believe are behind your thoughts. Lastly, name the emotions that accompany your thoughts.

Don't Compare Yourself to Others

You are unique. I know you probably rolled your eyes every time your loved ones told you this, but take it from a stranger, they're right! You have to claim your individuality if you want to stay sane, especially on social media. As you scroll through endless photos and reels, it's only a matter of time before you wish you were them. Who wouldn't? They have more money, the perfect body, and their dream job.

You're holding yourself to unrealistic standards when you compare yourself to people on social media. In the end, you're putting more pressure on yourself, which will suck away your joy.

One thing I find works well for those moments when I'm comparing myself to others and yearning for what they have is to practice gratitude. It's a simple, yet effective way, to be happy with yourself and what you have. It doesn't matter how little you have; when you take the time to discover things you're grateful for, you'll soon realize how much you actually have. Every breath you take is a reason to be grateful.

Instead of comparing yourself to someone else, measure up to the person you were yesterday and do all you can to grow as a person.

You're Going Through Big Changes

Transitioning into young adulthood is a time filled with a lot of change. You're leaving school and most probably your childhood home, as well. You have to make your own choices and take on new responsibilities. Your identity is developing, and with that, your sense of self is shifting.

Where you once looked to your teachers and parents as a way to validate your success, you now have to quantify your own value. This is challenging, and you may find yourself being extra sensitive to outside opinions before you find the sweet spot of taking to heart what others have to say, and what you believe to be true.

Self-love is especially important during times of transition or you may be too hard on yourself when you make mistakes as you step into your new life.

You Are Too Negative

If you dwell in negativity, you are the problem. That is the harsh reality. Criticism, rejection, discouraging experiences, and harmful situations are part of life. We all go through tough times, but it is how we handle them that makes the difference.

You can decide to spend time with all the thoughts and feelings that contribute to you feeling worthless, or you can actively attempt to find your self-worth. When you're stuck in a negative state of mind, you may have to admit that it's your own fault. I know that is hard to hear, but you're the one in control of your mind and how you react to events. In other words, it is up to you to shift your attention from thoughts and feelings that feed the "you're worthless" narrative.

Stop seeing the glass as either half empty or half full; pour it into a smaller glass, and the glass will be full. You should take such a positive approach with your thoughts and feelings too.

Now that you know some of the reasons that add fuel to the fire of worthlessness, we can look at what you can do when you forget your value.

1. Acknowledge What You're Feeling

They say the first step to change is acknowledging the problem. Feeling unworthy is a major problem and something you shouldn't ignore. Unfortunately, we often ignore it when we feel like nothing would change if we disappeared from the face of the earth— we don't acknowledge it, which means we can't challenge it.

Your life is not going to change unless you take a good, hard look at this feeling, and accept that it's there and that you can't hide from it. This is not the time to have a "this too shall pass" attitude. You need to address the root of your feeling of worthlessness, or you'll end up chasing short-term happiness in an attempt to forget your feelings. There's more to life than short bursts of happiness, so you need to look in the mirror and ask yourself, "What am I going to do about these feelings of worthlessness?"

2. Pay Attention to What Is Going On

The best way to get to the bottom of why you're feeling unworthy is to pay attention to what triggers this sentiment. It's as easy as being attentive to what is going on in your head.

Let's say you're having a bad day, instead of wallowing in negative emotions, think back to exactly when your day turned sour, or what happened to make you feel inferior. With this information, you can decide on a course of action. Maybe all you need to do is replace a self-deprecating thought with a compliment, or it could be that canceling plans with someone who makes you feel "less than" is the answer.

It's a skill to be so aware of your thoughts that you can notice them, analyze them, and move on, instead of being swept up in a tornado of negative self-talk.

3. Take Charge

So, you're feeling worthless. Who is going to change that? You! Yes, it is your responsibility to recognize your worth. It is your job to figure out why you're important.

You're accountable for your own happiness and success, but that also means you need to take responsibility for your unhappiness, failures, and feelings of insignificance.

It's only when you get out of the victim mentality that you'll be able to take complete ownership of your life. Taking responsibility requires courage and honesty, but it is something you'll have to do over and over again in life if you want to live authentically.

4. Celebrate the Little Things

No one is expecting you to walk right into a corner office and make millions. If that is something you're imagining, you may end up feeling worthless when you don't achieve this. So, start by being realistic. If you make plans that are unachievable in the timeframe you've set for yourself, you're setting yourself up to feel useless.

We're programmed to have dreams, and when we don't, we can't help but ask ourselves, "What am I even doing here?" To help you overcome this feeling, start small. Instead of aiming to double your income immediately, start by aspiring to cook yourself a meal or go to the gym three times a week; do something that proves you can start and complete your goals.

It's not possible for us to be perfect, but if you create habits of succeeding at the small stuff, you're much more likely to nail the big stuff too!

5. Appreciate What You Have

I can guarantee you that your feelings of worthlessness are baseless—you do contribute something to society. For one, your family and friends value you, and you mean a lot to them. But I know it's so easy to get lost in the challenges that we face.

You've probably recognized just how critical you are of yourself. Every single failure or setback makes you question your worth. During times like this, I want you to think of all the things you've already done. Dig around for something in your life you're really proud of and hold onto that memory until you feel better about yourself again.

THE POWER OF AFFIRMATIONS

I want to give you another tool to not only stand up to your inner bully but, to also help boost your self-esteem. Affirmations are a powerful tool to rewire your brain to be kinder to yourself. They help you challenge negative self-talk but, also have the ability to have a positive impact on your life in general. Think about it, when you're more confident, you're likely to believe in your abilities, and that will make it easier for you to say "Yes" to opportunities that can change your life for the better.

There are many people who don't understand how saying a few positive things to yourself daily can bring real change to your life. Believe me, affirmations aren't just wishful thinking. When done regularly, it's like exercising your brain, which changes your entire outlook. You end up internalizing statements that make you grow and don't hold you back because you question your worth.

If you're still unsure, try it out yourself. Commit to using affirmations for just one week, and you'll want to continue on because of the positive changes you'll experience. Here are three steps to help guide you as you get used to this transformative tool.

1. List the most common negative statements you make about yourself, but don't stop there. Add hurtful things other people have said to you that have had a lasting impact.
2. Now it is time to write down an affirmation that counters the negative statements you just listed. Use powerful words; for example, instead of saying, "I'm kind," say, "I'm a compassionate and caring person." Similarly, "efficient" and "accomplished" are two commanding words when you want to counter "incompetent" or "unable."
3. It's time to say your affirmations out loud. Choose a time of day that suits you. I prefer to do my

affirmations in the morning as it gives me the self-confidence to take the day by the horns. My husband, on the other hand, does it in the evening as a way to wipe away all the emotional gunk he gathered throughout the day. This way, he won't lie in bed replaying negative thoughts or comments people made. You can also look at yourself in the mirror to give affirmations some extra oomph, but it is not necessary.

How you do your daily affirmations isn't set in stone. Some people write notes and stick them throughout the house as random reminders, while others may ask a family member to help them through the process. It doesn't really matter how you do it. What is important is that you identify the undesirable thoughts that are damaging your state of mind and counter these thoughts with positive words of influence.

In this chapter, we covered the more philosophical side of who you are. In the next chapter, we're going to take a behind-the-scenes look at why you behave as you do.

KEY TAKEAWAYS

- Understanding values, principles, beliefs, ethics, and morals makes it easier for you to define your own, which brings you one step closer to becoming authentically you.
- Core values aren't affected by any outside forces, so if you know what yours are, you'll stay grounded.
- It takes a lot of courage to live life on your own terms.

- You should not underestimate the power self-love has on your life.
- You have an inner bully and they're very mean, but you can use affirmations to stand up to them.
- You have to feel good enough if you want to be good enough.

2

DEVELOP AND USE YOUR THINKING SKILLS

Creativity is not limited to artists, writers, or musicians—it is important to all of us if we want to improve our lives. Creative thinking is about connecting the dots. This pattern of thinking impacts all areas of your life but can come in especially valuable when you're applying for a job, as many companies prefer employees who can come up with innovative solutions to problems.

"Think outside of the box," is a phrase that children hear from a young age. Teachers and parents want their children to use their imagination to problem-solve, invent, or communicate. But how do you actually develop creative thinking skills?

In this chapter, you're going to learn to become a more innovative individual. It's easier than you think and before you know it, you'll be coming up with solutions to everyday challenges you'll face as you become an adult.

WHY CREATIVE THINKING IS ESSENTIAL

There are various types of thinking skills, each with its own pros and cons.

Convergent thinking: This is where you use your memory, logic, and resources to come up with the best answer to a problem.

Divergent thinking: This is the polar opposite of convergent thinking as there is no single correct answer to the problem; thinking of a solution or new idea is all that is required.

Critical thinking: This is all about analysis. You look at a problem or scenario and examine it to form a judgment about it and come up with a logical solution.

Creative or lateral thinking: This is when you take an unconventional approach to problem-solving. The aim is to approach an issue in an unusual way and from a perspective that hasn't been used before.

These thinking skills are vastly different but we use all of them to navigate the world. However, the transition that is currently taking place in your life requires a more imaginative approach, and that is why we're focusing on creative thinking.

Here is a list of reasons why it's recommended you be creative in your decision-making:

1. Your life and relationships become infinitely more beautiful as you inject a little bit of yourself into the world, and take a more creative approach to your daily dealings.
2. You'll become more confident as you use your creative thinking skills and will be more self-reliant as you notice you don't need to rely on others to solve problems for you.
3. You'll become more authentic. Creative thinking takes away any worry you may have about what other people are thinking, so you'll live a life more true to yourself.
4. You'll be more excited when you wake up in the morning as you'll be eager to come up with creative thoughts and ideas during the day.
5. You may discover some talents you didn't know you had as you use creative thinking to solve problems. Instead of nagging about the obstacles in your way, you can find new ways to overcome them.
6. You'll feel more fulfilled. There's nothing as horrible as experiencing life as dull and boring. When you think outside of the box, you'll train your brain to look for new challenges to explore and you'll never feel like you've achieved all you were meant to.
7. Creative thinking helps you master the challenges that you'll face. I'm not going to beat about the bush, I've been around a long time, and I still face trials and

tribulations, and so will you. That is why it is important to teach yourself skills to help you overcome difficult situations.

Taking a more creative approach to life will make you a happier person. If you're unsure how to apply creative thinking in your life, don't worry, I'm here to help.

The most important thing you should make sure of is that you feel uninhibited when you go through your thinking process. That's a great indication that you're applying creativity in your life.

Here are some ways you can be a creative thinker in all aspects of your life:

Take risks: Adventure is good for the soul. I'm not only talking about jumping from an airplane or scaling down a mountain. You can be adventurous in other ways. For example, going on a team-building weekend away with your coworkers is an adventure. Taking your boyfriend or girlfriend for a hike is an adventure. Life itself will also give you enough chances to use your creativity in an exciting way.

Don't be too serious: Yes, some problems you'll face won't leave room for you to playfully find a solution, but for those not-so-serious snags along the way, find the funny. Approaching certain problems in a lighthearted manner allows you to approach them in a creative way, which opens more opportunities to find a solution.

Keep thinking: When you're faced with a problem, don't hold back your mind. Think of all the possible solutions, however crazy they may sound. Before you know it, all the unique and unexpected thoughts may give you the answer you've been looking for.

Ask why: Being curious opens endless doors and possibilities. When you were around three or four, it's likely you drove your parents crazy by asking, "Why?" Tap into that energy just a little to coax out your creative side.

Read: Nurture your imagination. If you want to become a strong creative thinker, grab a book and immerse yourself in a world filled with inventiveness and inspiration.

If you follow these steps, gone are the days of limiting your possibilities by thinking in a narrow way. In other words, say "bye" to a boring you and "hello" to a creative thinker with a plan for every problem.

Another way to promote creative thinking is much like using the Sorting Hat in *Harry Potter*. Developed by Dr. Edward de Bono, the originator of the term "lateral thinking," the six sorting hats group your creative thinking into, you guessed it, six categories (De Bono, 2016). Let's break it down.

Thinking Hats

As mentioned, the six hats divide your thinking into six parts that are color-coded. When you know the type of thinking linked to each color hat, you can change your thought patterns from one hat to the other as needed.

Here are the colors of the six thinking hats and how you can use them to promote creative thinking:

Yellow hat: Your thoughts are positive, and you look for the silver lining in each situation.

White hat: You focus on the things you already know and the information you have at hand.

Blue hat: You look at the big picture.

Red hat: Take time to explore your feelings and emotions. Examine how you're reacting to the situation.

Green hat: Investigate your options. Look for alternative ways to approach the problem. Spend time creating new ideas.

Black hat: Even with creative thinking you have to be realistic about what can go wrong. Discover any possible difficulties you may face.

Creative thinking is when you make use of all the hats to help you think clearly and objectively. For example, you can put on the blue hat to figure out what exactly your objective is. It will give you an overall view of the situation. Next, you can put on the yellow hat to make sure your head is in the right space before you move on to the green hat to start working on a creative solution. You can then alternate between the red, white, and black hats. The red hat will help you keep track of what you're feeling, the white hat will make sure you use the knowledge you have to help you come up with a solution, and the black hat will be the voice reminding you of possible challenges you have to keep in mind.

Lateral thinking is freeing; it removes all the boundaries logical thinking has and gives you a chance to solve problems efficiently by exploring the unknown. Considering that we're mostly taught to be logical thinkers, we have to put in the effort to train our minds to be more creative. In addition, we need to learn how to jump from one hat to another as we attempt to solve problems.

There are, however, some things that get in the way of our creative thinking process. If you want to boost your creative thinking and live up to your full potential, here are some things you'll want to avoid to fully unleash your creativity.

Don't complain: You're wasting energy when you moan; instead, see problems on your path as opportunities to discover creative parts of yourself that are hidden within.

Get out of your comfort zone: It's easy to get stuck where you are because you feel safe there. You're not going to reach your full potential if you're not courageous enough to venture into unknown territory.

Forget what others think: I always tell my children that what others think of them is none of their business. You don't need to concern yourself with other people's judgment of you or how you live. The only person's opinion you should worry about is your own—if you're happy with who you are, own it.

Don't let others douse your creativity: You're not a robot, so don't let anyone treat you like one. Society is very much to blame for putting us in the boxes we're encouraged to "think outside of." It's up to you to fight for your right to be a creative, free-spirited, and unique individual. Don't stop your mind from exploring exciting places.

Leave your ego behind: Your ego is steadfast in its ways and will want you to be too. So, instead of worrying about who is right and who is wrong, shift your focus to what is right. When you remove your ego's influence on your thinking, you'll be more open-minded and will easily become a flexible thinker.

Don't hold back: There may be moments when you want to stay quiet instead of sharing an innovative idea. You're limiting yourself where you could be flourishing instead. I know you're afraid of ridicule but think about "what if." What if your idea ends up changing your life for the better?

Keep learning: The biggest piece of advice I can give you is to never stop learning. Pick up all the knowledge you can along the way—be like a sponge soaking up everything anyone has to teach you and then soak up some more information on your own too. The more you know, the easier it will be to put the creative solutions you come up with into practice.

FLEXIBLE THINKING

If you're not capable of adapting to change, you're going to find it difficult to navigate your way from being a young adult to being an adult. This is where flexible thinking comes in. It's a valuable skill to manage change and accept when things don't go your way.

Flexibility is about responding to change in a positive manner and changing your behavior in accordance with the situation or environment you find yourself in. You can also think of it as mental flexibility.

When you're not a flexible thinker, you may experience some reluctance to accept the changes you're now facing. To you, keeping things the same makes more sense—you want to do things the way you've always been doing them. You can imagine why this isn't a good frame of mind to have as you transition into adulthood.

Flexibility Is a Must

The real-world benefits of mental flexibility can't be overstated. Change is a reality, and there is no use in you fighting against it. Instead, you can develop skills that will help you cope with the ups and downs of life. What's more, you'll be better able to handle the stress that comes with being an adult.

When you don't work on your flexibility, you may experience the following:

- Frustration when even the smallest thing doesn't go as planned.
- Confusion when there are changes to schedules and routines.
- Repetition of the same mistakes.
- Inability to stick with something; instead, you'll jump from one activity to another or leave it altogether.
- Difficulty changing your point of view, no matter the amount of evidence that you're wrong.
- Breakdowns when rules change.

It's also worth noting that if you struggle with flexibility, there's a high likelihood that you'll find it difficult to plan, solve problems, and control your impulses and emotions. You'll also lack the ability to be mindful of your behavior and the impact it has on your environment. In other words, rigidity affects various aspects of your life, and you should do what you can to become more agile in thought.

As with most things, your attitude and environment will influence how you think. For example, when you're in an optimistic mood, your thinking will be broad and flexibility is more likely. On the flip side, if you're in an environment where you're fearful for whatever reason, your thinking will zone in on specific details, leaving no room for flexible thought. Ultimately, the ideal is to shift between mindsets based on what type of thinking is necessary.

Here are some strategies you can apply to improve your flexible thinking:

Change your setting: Go for a walk. Visit a coffee shop. Sit in the living room instead of in your bedroom. A change of scenery is like a breath of fresh air. You'll be able to feel the change in your thinking and that is exactly what we're looking for.

Question your thoughts: By now it is clear that your mind isn't always truthful—your inner critic has a way of twisting the truth in such a way that you feel worthless. For this reason, question your thoughts; don't just accept them blindly.

Take up a new hobby: Start dancing, learn a new language, or start to write a book. When you stimulate your brain, you improve your problem-solving abilities and become a more creative thinker—two things that make up an integral part of flexible thinking.

Break routine: This may be hard for you to do if you're not a flexible thinker, but it will help you overcome your need for planning and sticking to that plan. Start by being spontaneous in small areas of your day and work up to changing your routine in bigger ways.

When you follow these tips, your brain will become more malleable, and instead of wrestling with the inevitable changes you'll experience throughout life, you'll take them as they come. In the end, you'll go through life more peacefully, and reaching your goals won't be a source of constant stress.

CRITICAL THINKING

Although the focus of this chapter is chiefly on creative thinking, I think I would be amiss if I didn't include some information on critical thinking, as it does play a role in various aspects of your existence. Critical thinking keeps you rational—it helps you apply reason and logic to any problem.

If you're a critical thinker, you'll be able to make connections between ideas and will continuously question any assumptions you make. These are the big-picture thinkers who accept nothing at face value. In the end, critical thinking is all about finding the best solution to any problem.

Critical thinking is very much an "in the moment" type of thinking and not an accumulation of facts over time to come to a conclusion.

How would you react to a social media post doing the rounds claiming that your best friend did something questionable? If you're a critical thinker, you'd use rational thought, logic, and reason to assess how truthful the information is at the time.

Critical thinkers can:

- link ideas
- recognize, build, and weigh up various arguments
- take a systematic approach to finding solutions
- expose any disparities in assumptions and beliefs
- identify any inconsistencies and gaps in thinking

You now have a better understanding of what critical thinking is, but it will help you to know what specific process you need to follow.

1. Analysis

The first step is to think about the issue at hand objectively. When you do this, you get more clarity on exactly what the problem is.

2. Interpretation/Reflection

Now that you have a better idea about the issue, you can start to consider the different arguments pertaining to the matter.

Don't just look at one side; remember, critical thinking weighs up all arguments.

3. Evaluation

How strong are the different points of view? Which arguments are less valid than the others? Look for the weaknesses in the reasoning.

4. Inference

This step requires you to mull over the implications a decision will have on you and others.

5. Decision-Making/Problem-Solving

Lastly, it is time to organize your thinking in such a way as to support your final decision.

The main difference between creative and critical thinking is the structure linked to critical thought. There's no room for daydreaming and waiting for ideas to come to you; no, critical thinking requires active reasoning to reach a specific goal: to solve a problem or make a decision.

I always use solving a puzzle as the ultimate example of critical thinking—there's no room for creativity. The pieces fit together one way and one way only. Similarly, deciding to wear warm or cool clothes depending on the weather is another area where critical thinking is applied. How your clothing looks can include some creative thinking, but your decision to wear warm clothes when it is snowing outside comes down to critical thinking.

After reading this chapter and working on your creative thinking skills, you're going to have a much more laid-back approach to becoming independent. Although you'll have to make many decisions and solve various problems, you won't let it get you down. Going at it alone for the first time is usually an exciting time in any person's life, but it can be terrifying at the same time, especially if you're not equipped with the right thinking skills.

In the next chapter, we'll have a look at the practicalities of becoming more independent. We'll discuss some important things you need to know about owning a car and caring for a home so that you know what to expect.

KEY TAKEAWAYS

- Thinking outside the box is a skill that you should acquire if you want to live a more peaceful life.
- Creative thinking can help you become more genuine in your decision-making.
- You shouldn't feel repressed when making decisions; that's not going to lead to your happiness.
- Learn to hop between the six thinking hats when you're trying to creatively come to a solution.
- You need to be able to adapt to change; that is why flexible thinking is so important.

- Critical thinking is the opposite of creative thinking, but there will be times when you'll have to take a more logical approach to a problem.

3

INDEPENDENCE DAY

You've done it! You flew the nest and now you're ready to explore the big, wide world. This is definitely an exciting time in your life, but without the necessary skills, it can also be a stressful time.

Independent living skills will help you get through today, tomorrow, and the next but they don't come naturally—you pick these skills up from your parents and others as you grow up.

Below is a quick list of the type of skills I'm talking about. Tick them off as you read and you'll have a good indication of what you need to work on to make your transition to independent living easier.

You have to learn how to:

- understand nutritional information so that you can cook healthy meals
- keep your body fit and healthy
- keep your house neat and clean
- create and stick to a budget, pay your bills on time, and save money
- communicate effectively to get your point across
- get and keep a job
- behave at your workplace
- take care of your personal appearance
- maintain your house
- get along with others

Although this is not an extensive list, many of these skills are covered in this book and those that aren't, your parents or other adults will be able to help you with.

If you grew up in an unstable home, with parents who weren't financially stable, didn't take care of their health, and didn't look after the house or their belongings, it is understandable that it will be more challenging for you to master some of these skills. Keep trying; breaking the cycle is possible.

Many believe your generation has it too easy. One study found that one in four young adults has moved back in with their parents after they failed to live independently (Pew Research Centre, 2012). This shows that your generation is unprepared to deal with what life has to throw at them. Young adults who end up back at their parents' home tend to feel unworthy and they lose self-esteem. It's not nice to rely on others to care for you when you're totally capable of doing so yourself. The aim of this chapter is to give you enough knowledge to make a success of your life without ever having to rely on your parents to look after you again.

So, let's look at how we can prepare you for living on your own.

GET EDUCATED

I'm not talking about going to college and further educating yourself—that goes without saying. I want you to get as much knowledge as you can about life and live it in a way that honors your purpose. Learn about yourself—mind, body, and soul—and then learn some more.

There is so much wisdom out there; books written by people who have dedicated their lives to figuring out how to exist in such a way that when you lay your head down on your pillow at night, you feel grateful and content, ready to take on tomorrow with the same vigor.

You should also ask your parents, grandparents, or any other person who has lived a long and happy life for their advice. I know when you're young, you think you have it all figured out, but the sooner you realize that's not true, the less time you'll waste telling those with more life experience that you don't need their guidance.

When you soak up all the information you can, you're taking responsibility for your life and actions. You can't plead ignorance when you make the wrong decision or do something that's out of character if you have all this knowledge at your fingertips.

Never stop learning and always try to better yourself. If we don't constantly work on doing better and becoming more, what are we even doing here?

ON THE JOB

If you're still studying or you haven't found a job yet, don't worry, the time is coming. But you have to ask yourself if you are looking for "just a job" or a career. For many, being a waiter or delivering pizzas is "just a job"—something they do to save up for a car or to pay for accommodation while they're studying. They don't plan on doing this for their whole life, but they are using it as a financial stepping stone until they can start their career.

Now, I do have to mention that being a CEO of a big company can also be seen as "just a job." This usually happens when someone isn't doing something they feel passionate about. Maybe they were forced to go the business route when they actually wanted to do something more creative. Whatever the case may be, there are two things you have to ask yourself before you go looking for a job.

1. What am I good at?
2. What do I love doing?

When you answer these two questions, you'll be able to find a balance between your talents and your passions and this is what sets apart having a career from having just a job.

Find a Job You Want

A big chunk of your day is spent at the office or traveling to and from work. Then there are the times when you're home and you can't stop thinking about an approaching deadline, or worse yet, your boss keeps hounding you even on your days off. Can you imagine being stuck in a job that has no purpose for you? Frustration, anxiety, depression, and burnout will surely follow. You'll dread getting up in the morning and live for weekends when you'll be too tired and run down to do anything you enjoy anyway.

I don't want to scare you, but finding satisfaction at work is essential if you want to live a happy life. Of course, not all of us can combine what we love with what we do for a living, so we have to work a little harder to find meaning in our work. Thankfully, it is possible.

Basically, you have three options:

1. You find a job that aligns with your passion right off the bat.
2. You look for ways to find purpose in a job that you don't really love.
3. You change your career path and find a job you're passionate about.

Number one is the ultimate choice, but at least you have two more options to choose from to help make such an important part of your life more bearable.

Below are tips to help you find a job that you're passionate about.

Tip #1

The first thing you have to do is research jobs that match your interests. You may be surprised that many careers include things you're passionate about. If you're still in the dark regarding what excites you jobwise, then I recommend you use an online career test to help you discover your passions. There are various quizzes, questions, and personality assessments that will identify careers best suited to you.

When you have a list of possible careers, do some research. Find out more about the industry, common positions, average salaries, and growth possibilities. This will answer a lot of questions that will help you when you make your final decisions.

You should also talk to others currently employed in your perfect position. Ask them questions to get a real sense of what the job entails and then decide if it meets your expectations or not.

Tip #2

Now that you have a general idea of what jobs you find interesting, you should take time to see what skills you have and don't have. As you're just starting out, your skill pool won't be that large, but it will give you an idea of how much you still have to learn before applying for the position. Also, don't forget to list skills like hard-working, honesty, and drive. Those skills matter too!

Tip #3

Okay, so you lack some skills; don't feel despondent! There are many ways you can upskill. You can attend extra classes, or volunteer to work as an intern to gain valuable experience. I suggest you use the time to not only gain new abilities but to also make sure you enjoy the career you plan on pursuing.

Tip #4

If you fancy yourself an entrepreneur, you can start your own business. This way you'll know that you're doing something that drives you and awakens your passion. The best yet is that you won't need to answer to anyone else but yourself and your business partners or investors. I do have to warn you that starting your own business is easier said than done. It is going to take a lot of planning if you want it to be successful. Getting your dream financed is also a headache, so if you plan on going this route, you have to face the reality that you'll have to overcome many obstacles—and you're going to work ten times harder in the beginning.

Tip #5

Pace yourself. It's easy to get overwhelmed when you start a job for the first time. I know you want to impress everyone by jumping in and doing not only your work but anyone else's who is willing to give it to you! Stop. If you jump all in from day one, you're going to burn out and that can lead to you having to take sick days, making unnecessary mistakes, having a short fuse with your colleagues, and other negative consequences. Take care of yourself or stress will get the better of you and a job you once loved can quickly turn into one you hate.

Communication in the Workplace

In Chapter 5, there's a section about communication in general, but I feel it is appropriate to focus on the importance of communication in the workplace. Although there is some overlap, communication in the workplace is essential for career advancement.

It doesn't matter if you're an intern or the CEO of a company, strong communication skills are needed to build and maintain working relationships. If there aren't open lines of communication, there's no trust and, this will affect morale negatively, which will decrease productivity.

When you're an effective communicator, you listen to understand and, take time to respond in an engaged and considerate manner. If you're the one doing the talking, you speak in a clear and confident manner, and you're always polite in your interactions.

We live in a digital age and that means that you have to also consider how you communicate via email and other digital platforms. Without effective communication with your colleagues, staff, or supervisors, it will be nearly impossible for you to achieve success in a working environment.

Let's look at some communication skills you can start using during the interview and after you get the job!

Office Communication Skills

Working on your communication skills is a surefire way to stand out from the rest. When you go for a job interview, recruiters have already seen your resume; now it is time for you to dazzle them with a neat and well-put-together appearance, and most importantly, top communication skills. If you follow the skills listed below and combine them with those you'll learn in Chapter 5, the way forward will be paved with good things. Of course, once you're hired, continue working on your communication skills!

Listen

You may believe that communication is all talk, talk, talk. You'd be wrong. People who excel at communication know how to listen. To them, it's a matter of listening only enough so that they can put in their two cents. You need to practice active listening if you want to be a top communicator. It's easier than you think. All you have to do is pay attention when someone else is talking. Don't dig around in your head for responses but focus on the words and sentences coming out of their mouth. Ask questions if you don't understand something and, when you do understand, rephrase what was said so that the other person sees you're trying to comprehend what they're saying.

Be Friendly

No one wants to communicate with someone who is rude, unsociable, and hostile. So make sure your tone is friendly and there's a smile on your face when you're having a chat with your coworkers. Being polite is essential in the workplace—face-to-face as well as in written communication. Asking a personal question (not too personal, though) or sharing something about your life outside of work is a good way to engage in friendly and open conversation. When writing emails, you can personalize things somewhat with, "I hope you had a great weekend," thrown in somewhere. This will make the recipient feel that you actually care for and appreciate them.

Have Empathy

Active listening is a must if you want to respond with empathy; you can't honestly say, "I understand what you mean," if you didn't actually hear what they said. That type of dishonesty will cause distrust and that is the last thing you want in the workplace. Listen and then step into their shoes so that you can truly understand where they're coming from.

Even when you and your boss or coworker aren't on the same page, it is still important to be understanding of their point of view and respect their opinion.

Exude Confidence

If you're not self-assured while you're talking, how can you expect anyone to get on board with what you're saying? You have to be confident when you communicate to show others that you believe in what you're saying. A good example of communicating confidently is avoiding statements that sound like questions. Your body language (more on that in Chapter 5) is also a great way to convey sureness.

Do make sure that you don't confuse confidence with arrogance or aggression; it's a very fine line.

Stay Open-Minded

There's no room for rigidity if you want to be a great communicator. Approach any conversation with an open mind. Think of it as a give-and-take exchange. Listen and understand, but don't shy away from sharing your opinion. The key is to remember that there is a difference between sharing your beliefs and trying to force them down someone else's throat.

Ultimately, honest and productive conversations are made up of back-and-forth dialogue; you're not giving a speech.

Pick the Right Communication Channel

You'd be surprised how many people choose the wrong form of communication. For example, breaking up with someone over text or email is pretty frowned upon, and for good reason. Similarly, you don't fire someone or change their salary by sending them an email. Certain things are meant to be done in person.

Think about the importance or severity of what you want to convey, and then choose the appropriate channel. Also, consider how much time the person has; if you want to have a face-to-face chat with your boss about something, they may get annoyed because you're wasting their time when you could've just sent an email. Give thought to your means of communication and the recipient will receive and respond in a more positive light.

How to Develop the Skills

If you're on a mission to develop your communication skills, the first thing you can do is observe how others converse and the reactions that follow. For example, if you see Bill is being condescending and rude, have a look at how Emily reacts. Depending on her personality, she'll either become quiet and look sad, or she'll get angry and stand up to Bill, which will escalate matters. Whatever her reaction, one thing is sure, it was negative and influenced by Bill's lack of communication skills. Now you know what not to do. Being a keen observer gives you an insight into workplace dynamics.

You can also look into formal education. A master's degree in communication is an option if you're very interested in how interactions in the office impact career growth and the functioning of a business. It will also open up a number of doors for you, including increased job opportunities, an increase in salary, job security, and much more.

GOALS

I mentioned having goals, in short, earlier, but it is a vital part of life that many people neglect, so we have to equip you with some tools.

Many of us go through life on autopilot. We get so caught up in the same routine that we forget what we really want. Some of us know what we want, but we don't know how to get there. This is where goal setting comes in handy.

Benjamin Franklin said, "If you fail to plan, you are planning to fail," and that is absolutely true (Goodreads, n.d.). The biggest part of planning is setting goals—not only your final goal, but mini goals along the way that build toward you reaching your ultimate objective, whatever that may be. In other words, you need to set goals if you want to succeed in life.

Any skill you want to develop, from forming and maintaining relationships right to learning how to lead a team, are goals in and of themselves. Goal setting is based on the idea that consciously setting objectives influences your actions (Ryan, 1970). Also, if it is a noteworthy goal, you'll try harder to achieve it and your chances of success will improve.

Why and How to Set Goals

When you successfully complete a goal, you get a surge of dopamine—one of the hormones responsible not only for making you feel happy, but also for making you feel motivated. So, after reaching one goal, you'll want to take on the next and the next, and so on until you reach your greatest goal, whatever that may be.

All this success will boost your self-efficacy and self-confidence. As you can see, goal setting has a profound effect on your life in so many ways, and if you want to be victorious, there are five key principles you need to apply (Locke & Latham, 1990).

1. Commitment

It's no use setting a goal you're not dedicated to achieving. You're going to face obstacles along the way because things hardly ever go as planned; for that reason, you need to be 110% committed to giving it your all.

With the right amount of dedication, you'll be able to see when your effort is inadequate and then try a little harder to attain your goal. How committed you are matters even more when you're trying to pull off a challenging goal—you're more likely to give up if you're not steadfast.

One aspect that influences a person's commitment level is how much they desire what they're working toward. If it's not something you really want, then why would you dedicate your time and energy to achieving it?

2. Clarity

What exactly are you hoping to achieve? You have to be very specific if you want to be successful. If your goal is too vague, you're likely to lose motivation as you work toward it. However, if a goal is clear and measurable, you'll understand what you have to do, and this will result in you accomplishing what you set out to achieve.

3. Challenging

I don't know about you, but I get bored very quickly if I do something that doesn't challenge me in some way. If your goal is too undemanding, you'll underperform and lose interest. Our motivation is driven by achievement (small goals along the way) and the anticipation of achievement (ultimate goal).

4. Complexity

Just as a goal that's too simple will impede your success, so too will goals that are too complex. You need to set goals that are attainable. In other words, you need the skill and capability to actually achieve your goals. If you don't, you may get frustrated, despondent, and overwhelmed, which will negatively impact your motivation and productivity.

5. Feedback

When others comment on your progress, you'll be able to determine how you are progressing. You can use this as a guide to which areas you should improve in, and how. When you feel you're advancing toward your goal at an adequate pace, you may be inclined to learn a new skill to help you progress even faster. You may also set more challenging goals as time goes on and the feedback you get is positive.

If your goals are more personal in nature, it won't be possible for you to get feedback from others—unless you share your dreams with someone. Luckily, internal feedback is just as helpful as gathering outsiders' thoughts.

Skills Required to Set Goals

We've had a look at the principles that apply to goal setting, but you also require certain skills for successful goal setting. If you've struggled to achieve your goals in the past, it is likely that you lacked one or more of these skills. Don't worry; the abilities you need can easily be learned and developed through practice.

Planning: You need to plan properly if you want to achieve your goals. This means you have to be able to prioritize and organize your "to-do" lists in such a way that you maintain focus.

Self-Motivation: You have to be your own cheerleader. I know you may have others rooting for you, but they're not the ones who actually have to put in all the work and stay motivated. This is why self-motivation is crucial. What's more, with adequate motivation, you won't mind acquiring new skills to help you succeed.

Time Management: Goal setting and time management go hand in hand. There should always be a timescale and deadline, or you may get stuck at a specific sub-goal, and eventually, you'll lose focus entirely. We'll have a more in-depth look at time management later on.

Self-Regulation: Emotional regulation is a valuable skill in life. You need to be able to regulate your own emotions—and in the case of goal setting in a work environment, others' emotions, as well. Managing emotions forms part of your emotional intelligence, which makes it possible for you to describe your goals in a clear and concise way.

Flexibility: Things don't always go as planned. How you deal with sudden changes or obstacles will be a determining factor in whether or not you'll succeed. You need to roll with the punches and persevere to reach your goal.

Strategies for Goal Setting

We've covered the most important aspects of goal setting and specified the skills you need to develop to make sure you achieve success. Lastly, I want to share some strategies with you that—in combination with what you've read above—will make the process of setting objectives more straightforward.

Brainstorm: Earlier, we discussed your core values and how you can use them to guide you toward your purpose. Sit down and think about what you want to achieve; be specific and add as much detail as you can. When you have clear goals, you will have a better idea of what you need to do to achieve them. Write all this down, but take your time to think about what you really want.

Create a map to success: Working toward a goal is a journey, and most journeys have a map to help you get there. Take the time to plot the way toward your final destination. This is a great way to activate logical thinking. One example you can use is a goal tree. Right at the top, you'll write down your end goal; below that, you'll list between four and six mini goals that you'll need to achieve to reach your final objective. Under the mini goals, you'll write down the conditions necessary to achieve each.

Believe in yourself: You have to have confidence in your abilities, but in the same breath, if things don't go according to plan, you have to be willing to reevaluate things. When you're overly confident, you may not notice when you've lost direction and it may take you longer to reach your goals.

Stay accountable: When you tell others about your goals, you'll be more inclined to stay committed to achieving them. Let's say you tell a family member about your goals and the next time you see them, they ask you how it is going. It's not going to feel very good if you have to admit that you haven't been working on it.

If you apply these goal-setting tips, you're setting yourself up for success. Now it's time to have a closer look at time management to help increase your chances of reaching your goals.

TIME MANAGEMENT

Learning to manage your time now will help you in the future. Life has a tendency to become more complicated as you get older. Your dream job may be further away from your home than your current one, so traveling there steals more of your time. This means you will have to either give up one activity you used to do in your extra time, or you'll have to make time for it during your day.

The ability to adjust your time is a skill that will take a lot of practice. You will need to learn to prioritize your to-do list and to stick to a schedule if you want to get around to doing everything you need to. Time management and productivity are best friends, and together they open up a world of drive and motivation. That sounds like the ultimate recipe for success.

You'll soon discover that time is a valuable commodity—and although many say, "Time is money," in many instances, time is more valuable. If you want to effectively reach your goals, you have to be intentional and disciplined. This is particularly difficult for young adults like yourself. You have a lot more freedom as you venture out into the adult world; your school and parents don't manage your schedules and priorities any longer.

If I can give you one time management tip, it would be to take the time to prioritize worthwhile ways to spend your time. You have to decide what is important and what isn't. If you don't, you may find yourself being very busy but getting nowhere. If you don't move closer to your goals in a productive way, you'll become frustrated and disappointed.

Of course, I'm not going to give you only one time management tip. Although prioritizing is of utmost importance, there are other strategies you should employ to make sure you don't waste a minute.

Don't Multitask

If you do more than one thing at a time, surely you're getting a lot done in a short period of time, right? Although that is true in theory, in practice you're actually less productive when you're constantly switching from one task to another. The likelihood of making mistakes also increases because, while you're working on one thing, you're thinking of another. In other words, you may end up wasting time, since you'll have to circle back and fix any mistakes.

Take Breaks

You may think that taking a break is a waste of time, but you have to remind yourself that you're not a robot; you need to revitalize your mind so you can focus again. You'll make fewer mistakes if you schedule a break every now and again because you'll give your brain time to rest and get ready for the next spurt of concentration. The secret is to not do something you enjoy too much or you may find it hard to stop and get back to work.

Log Your Time

You need to discover time wasters. One way to do this is to write down what you're doing every 15 minutes. Do this for one week and you'll be able to see what consumes most of your time. You can then decide if you need to eliminate some things or reprioritize your daily tasks entirely.

Ask for Help

Sometimes, we take on more than we can chew. If this is the case, ask for help. Have a look at all the things you need to do each day and see which of these tasks you can trust others to do. Also, keep in mind that those around you may have skills that will come in handy in completing some tasks. There's nothing wrong with asking for help, but don't forget that they have a schedule of their own, so don't take up too much of their time.

Stay Organized

A calendar is your best friend when it comes to time management. If you organize your regular tasks, you'll know exactly what times you have open to focus on the other things you need to do. Having a scheduling conflict is a massive waste of time, not only for you, but the other person.

Managing your time isn't easy, but it is necessary. As you age, you may start to feel that there aren't enough hours in the day to do all the things you want or need to do. Add to that the fact that you have much more to do now than when you were a teenager, and finding time for it all seems nearly impossible. The good news is that you can get more done if you work on your time management skills. If you follow the strategies above, you may even have a few minutes left in the evening for some "me time"!

HEALTHY HABITS

Habits can be a good or bad thing. Some people repeat bad habits even though it is harmful to their well-being. Then there are people who form habits that improve their lives. Whatever the case may be, the saying "old habits die hard" is true, and that is why you should make sure you fall into a routine that is advantageous to your life plan. Building habits that lead to growth while you're still young is a great way to set yourself up for long term greatness.

Here are some habits you should build as a young adult:

Learn to Cook

This goes without saying since you need to eat to survive, but you'll be surprised how many people in their twenties have no idea how to prepare meals. They might know how to fry an egg and make toast, but that's about as far as it goes. This creates a problem as they'll eat out or buy fast food on the go—which means their wallet will get thinner and their waistline thicker.

There are many recipes for you to find online and even videos that show you, step-by-step, what to do. Once you know the basics, you can start to experiment and, before you know it, you'll be able to create gourmet meals and save money doing so.

Travel... a Lot

There's something about traveling that expands your outlook on life. You experience so many new things and learn to appreciate people and their cultures. Taking a break from your daily routine also gives you a new perspective.

I know travel can be expensive, but if you work smart, you can see the world inexpensively. For example, you can look for group deals, since the costs are usually lower when there are more people traveling. You can also look for cheap lodgings, like Airbnbs or hostels. If you want to travel far, there are various third-world countries where our dollar can be stretched much farther. I would like to caution you to have safety in mind when you're traveling. Nothing can ruin your adventure faster than having someone steal your wallet or purse. Keep your ID and money in a travel pouch that you can hide under your clothes. Also, make sure to travel in groups, or at the very least pairs, to avoid being mugged or hurt. Avoid being in an isolated area; always stay where there are lots of people, and, if you do find yourself alone, in an unfamiliar area, and you see potential trouble, make a lot of noise to get the attention of anyone who might be in the area who can lend assistance. Don't think you have to go abroad; I'm sure there are many sights and places to see that are reasonably close to you.

Don't Look for Love

If you're a fan of watching romcoms, you may mistakenly believe that life is a quest to find Mr. or Ms. Right. Although these movies almost always have a happy ending, in reality, it's not that easy to find your soulmate and live happily ever after. You may want to jump onto social media, join dating apps, or go out as much as you can to meet possible love interests, but take a breath. Love shouldn't be your main focus now. You should use this time to develop a growth mindset, focus on building a career, and figure out your purpose.

Date… a Lot

I know it may sound like I'm contradicting myself, but bear with me. There's a difference between actively searching for someone to marry and have babies with, and dating someone to have fun with—and no, I'm not talking about having sex. You can enjoy a meal at a great restaurant, go to a live concert together, visit the zoo, or do other fun things together. Think of dating as making a friend who may or may not turn into your life-long partner. This is the time of your life and you should enjoy it.

Don't Look for Happiness

We often get so caught up in what we assume happiness is: fast cars, big houses, lots of money. In reality, true happiness comes from the inside. You have to be content with what you have and where you're at in this particular moment. I'm not saying you should settle, but you should be grateful for your circumstances and foster a sense of contentment even if you want to continue improving.

Happiness is not your next pay increase, buying your first car, or finding your soulmate; those are just fleeting moments of joy. Work toward self-acceptance, having a positive outlook, and being grateful, and you'll get happier by the day—and best yet, this type of happiness is long-term!

Drink More Water

I'm not joking; drinking enough water is a life-changing habit. So many people walk around dehydrated. This means their body is holding onto toxins, which will undoubtedly make them feel ill. Water is a requirement for many bodily functions and if you don't consume enough, your body will have to find a way to overcompensate for your negligence. How? Well, you may crave coffee, or feel hungry when you're actually just thirsty. Give your body what it needs and it will give you its best.

Read

No one is too busy to read, especially not in this day and age with audiobooks and reading apps. The knowledge you take in when you read broadens your perspective, develops your brain, and improves your vocabulary. No wonder some of the most successful people in the world, like Elon Musk, Richard Branson, Oprah, and the late Steve Jobs, are known to read a lot.

Exercise

The unfortunate reality is you're not a teenager anymore, and as you get older, your body will naturally start to deteriorate. If you want to slow down the decline, you need to exercise every day. Get up earlier in the morning and do a 30-minute workout. You don't have to join a gym if you don't want to; going for a brisk walk or a jog in the neighborhood is more than sufficient as long as it's for 30 minutes or longer. Weight management will also be easier if you're active daily; this is especially true if you have a desk job where you sit most of the time.

Eat Healthily

What you fuel your body with matters. If you teach yourself healthy eating habits from early on, you can prevent many diseases linked to unhealthy eating. Get out of the mindset that eating greens are gross—they're some of the most nutritious foods on the planet! You're not a child anymore, so being fussy about what you eat isn't an option any longer. Food is fuel and if you think of it that way, you'll be less inclined to focus only on how things taste but rather on what they can do for your health. If you really can't stomach eating your greens, try drinking it by making yourself a green smoothie to kickstart your day. By the way; your taste buds will soon acquire an appreciation for the foods you use to avoid.

Creating new habits isn't as hard as you may think. The key is not to overdo it; focus on forming one new habit at a time, and take your time to master it. Take a month and get used to this new routine. Of course, there will be times when you'll mess up, but that's to be expected. Keep trying even if you have to take baby steps.

LET'S GET PRACTICAL

Some aspects of living independently require a hands-on approach. You'll have possessions or assets that require you to look after them in a specific manner if you want them to last, or retain (even grow) in value. In this section, we're going to focus on caring for your car and maintaining your apartment or house. We're also going to look at how to deal with emergencies—believe me, you don't want to run around like a headless chicken in a moment where absolute concentration and clarity can save a life.

I'm excited for you. Being a responsible adult includes looking after your belongings, and you know what? You get this feeling of pride if you care for your things—it's hard to explain, but I have no doubt you'll experience it if you follow the instructions below.

How to Care for Your Car

You may have been using your mom or dad's car for the last few years, so apart from keeping their car clean and not crashing it, proper car care wasn't really your job. Now that you're moving out and starting life on your own, you're probably looking to buy a new car—if you haven't already.

Buying a car is an investment, and if you want to increase its value for when you want to trade up, keeping it in tip-top condition is a must (DeBruhl, 2023).

According to DeBruhl, here are the top things you need to know:

- The owner's manual is one of the most important documents you'll ever get, relating to your car. It contains all the information you will ever need and has answers to the most common questions. Have a read-through it to familiarize yourself with the mechanics of your car. It can be nerve-wracking when you turn on the ignition and you're faced with flashing lights and beeps that you don't know the meaning of.
- Replace your windshield wipers when they're not doing a good job of swiping away rain and snow anymore. Make sure you buy blades that fit your car. If you're unsure, check with the car dealership on wiper blades made specifically for your car.
- Change your air filter every 12,000 or so miles. You can pay a professional to do it, or if you like to tinker with cars, you can attempt it yourself. You can look at the owner's manual to find out where it is positioned, and sometimes even some instructions on how to change it. Changing the air filter will save you money in the long run.
- To make sure there is a good connection between your battery and your car, clean the battery terminals regularly. Think of the battery as your car's nervous system—it plays an integral role in how it functions, so do what you can to prevent corrosion. Put on some gloves and protective eyeglasses before pouring a solution of water and baking soda on the terminals. You

can then scrub it with a wire brush until the foam is clear.
- Spray a commercial degreaser on your engine and rinse with water. This not only cleans your engine but is an opportune moment to check for leaks. Again, if you're not one to get your hands dirty, there are professionals who will help you at a price.
- Minor scratches happen but luckily you can touch up the exterior paint of your car. You will get an exact color match if you buy it from the car dealership.
- The condition of your tires is vitally important. Check the tread and immediately replace your tires when they're worn down—your life is at stake if you don't. Also, if you want to get better fuel mileage, check the air pressure before every long journey.
- If you somehow tear the upholstery in your car—hey, accidents happen—use a vinyl or leather patch kit to repair it. If you don't get an upholstery needle in the kit, I recommend you go to a fabric or craft store to buy one. They're strong enough to do the job.
- Mix up some toothpaste, baking soda, and water and apply it to your headlight surface to get rid of the cloudiness.
- Check the oil and water levels of your car at least every three weeks.

That covers the most important minor maintenance aspects of taking care of a car. Of course, you want to service your car according to the maintenance plan you have with the dealership where you bought the car.

One last matter I want to address is loaning out your vehicle. You may want to help someone in need, and that is very noble, but it is best to find another way to assist them. If something happens while they're in possession of your car—they get into an accident or your car gets stolen—you're the one who will have to deal with the consequences. Instead of lending them your car, offer to pay for their Uber or Lyft. And remember, if they don't have the money for a car of their own, they won't have the money to replace yours if they wreck it!

Owning your own car is a privilege; do your best to keep it. Most of all, enjoy the freedom that comes with being able to get around on your own!

How to Care for a Home

So, you've done it—you packed up all your belongings and now you're on your way to your new living space. It doesn't matter if you're living in a dorm, sharing an apartment with friends, or renting a place on your own, there are some things you need to consider before living on your own.

First, you have to keep in mind that your environment influences your success. In other words, if you're rooming with party animals, you'll have to deal with noise, a lot of people in your space, and the peer pressure to get rowdy with your roomies. If you're someone who likes a quiet and clean space, this may not be the best living setup for you. Your mind will also be calmer, and more focused, when you live in a place that's calm and where everything is orderly.

With that in mind, property maintenance is something you'll have to do at one point or another if you want to keep calling a place your home. If you're not a "do it yourselfer" you can get outside help, but some of these issues are minor and simple enough for you to take care of. Who doesn't like to save some money?

Here are some common issues you may encounter and how you can fix them:

Power outlet is not working: Sometimes it's as simple as a breaker tripping. If one of the outlets isn't working, check the breaker and flip the switch if something tripped. Voila! Power! How easy was that?

Moisture trapped in the bathroom: If there's no place for steam to escape, your health is in danger as moisture buildup can lead to black mold. If you notice that your bathroom stays steamy for a long time after you have a shower or take a bath, check your vents. Sometimes lint and debris get stuck in there and prevents proper airflow. One tip is to take a piece of tissue or toilet paper and hold it in front of the vent to see if there's movement.

Toilet isn't flushing: Grab a plunger and see if that works. It's a big no-no to flush wipes or feminine hygiene products as they will clog everything, and you may come face-to-face with an overflowing toilet—not for those with weak stomachs, for sure! The toilet should be reserved for Nos. 1, 2, and 3 (usually happens after a night out with friends or a bad batch of tortillas) and toilet paper.

A/C not working as it should: Check the filters. Much like the vents in your bathroom, your A/C filter can get clogged. If you clean it out, the air will flow, and it will function correctly. You need to replace the filter at times. It is suggested to do this every month for peak efficiency.

These are a few simple things you can try and fix yourself before asking for help. Why pay for professional service if it is something you could've done yourself to begin with?

Handling Emergencies

Listen to Murphy: If something can happen, it probably will (unless you're prepared). Life comes with a lot of surprises, including emergency situations where you need to man or woman up and save lives. Knowing what to do in emergencies will help you keep calm in a situation that would otherwise cause confusion and panic.

In this section, we will prepare you for dealing with an emergency.

Assess the Situation

It's true that emergencies require you to act fast, but it's no use if you end up doing things that make the situation worse. First, you need to keep calm; as soon as you feel overwhelmed, confused, or anxious, stop and take a moment to gather your thoughts. Take a few breaths and give yourself time to calm down. Remember, if there are other people, they will need your calmness to be able to overcome the panic they're experiencing.

When you have composed yourself, decide if there's something you can help with. If there's nothing you can do other than calling for emergency assistance, then that is okay. You can still remain calm and take control of the situation until trained rescue personnel arrive on the scene. If you have the necessary knowledge to help the injured person, do your best with what you have. Just remember that you should never attempt to move them in any way or you risk them being paralyzed.

If the emergency is of such a nature that you and others are in danger—a chemical spill, bomb threat, mass shooting—get yourself to safety. If you can help others leave the area, that would be a kind thing to do.

Be Prepared

The best way to handle an emergency situation is to be as prepared as you can be. Create an emergency plan with steps to follow in any given danger. With a plan in place, you'll save valuable time doing what is necessary to save your life and others' lives as well.

Keep a first aid kit in your house, but take it one step further by taking a course that teaches you how to use everything included in the kit. If you know to properly apply compresses, bandages, and tourniquets, you can keep someone alive long enough for the paramedics to arrive. I recommend you also learn how to do cardiopulmonary resuscitation (CPR) in the event that you witness someone having a heart attack.

911 is not the only important number you need to know during an emergency. Other medical phone numbers, including your

doctor's number and that of your next of kin, should be kept next to the phone. This isn't only for you to use, but will also help emergency response personnel if you're the one in need of help and they have to reach your family. You can also add the number of the poison control center if you live in an area with dangerous creepy crawlies.

If you have any allergies or chronic health conditions, you won't be able to let anyone know in case of an emergency where you're unconscious. For this reason, you should wear a medical ID tag so that people can have access to your information when you're unable to share it with them. This can save your life.

This was a mammoth chapter, but suddenly having to care for yourself is an enormous responsibility and you need all the help you can get. And we're not done yet! In the next chapter, we're talking about money management. I don't want to put a damper on your newfound freedom, but you should learn to spend money wisely as soon as you put your foot out of your childhood home—if you haven't already mastered it while still in school. Believe me, you'll thank yourself later in life.

KEY TAKEAWAYS

- Education isn't limited to learning institutions. You have to learn from the school of life as well if you want to transition from a young adult to a successful adult.

- You have to decide if you want "just a job" or to build a career. That will determine the steps you need to take to get employed.
- Job satisfaction is absolutely essential if you want to get out of bed each morning with a spring in your step. If you hate your job, you're going to hate your life.
- Communicating in the workplace is slightly different from communicating with friends and family. You have to master this skill if you want to advance in your career.
- Set goals or you will go through life on autopilot.
- There are not enough hours in the day to get everything done, so you have to prioritize your to-do list and manage your time or else you'll fall behind.
- Creating positive habits that will help you grow as a human will set you up for greatness. A habit as simple as drinking enough water or eating a healthy meal is something small you can do that will have a big impact.
- You're independent now and will have to learn how to take care of your car and look after the place you're living. If you attempt to do what you can yourself, you'll save money.
- Prepare for emergencies and you'll be able to stay calm if you find yourself in such a situation one day.

BECOMING AN ADULT IS INEVITABLE BUT THE PATH IS NOT ALWAYS A SMOOTH ONE!

"One of the greatest struggles of becoming an adult is figuring out what you want to do and what makes you happy. The courageous thing is to stick with it and see it through and see if you were correct."

— KRISTEN STEWART

Adulthood is a rite of passage that offers so many exciting things just within your reach. It's a time when high school is coming to an end, and you might be driving and experiencing freedom. And, of course, your voice can be heard now that you can legally vote. There might even be some financial independence with your first part-time job.

What is not to like about becoming an adult?

Well, each of these amazing experiences comes with its own set of challenges. High school is coming to an end but you are under immense pressure to get the grades you need to follow your dreams. The car that gives you freedom needs maintenance. Your first job is a great experience for your resume, but have you got the right time management skills—not to mention money management skills?

Nobody told you that becoming an adult was such a double-edged sword! While your brain is full of academic knowledge that will help you pass exams, there is little education on how to glide through this giant transition. The stress and anxiety can quickly take over your entire life. It doesn't have to be this way. You might not have reached the legal age of being an adult just yet, but that doesn't mean you can't start getting ahead now. But there is another way you can make a difference.

Taking just a couple of minutes to leave a review will help other young people take control with the essential life skills and guidance in this book.

There are approximately 21.56 million young people in the U.S. aged between 15 and 19. Although you may feel alone, each of them will be going through something similar to what you are right now.Get your voice heard by sharing your opinions – you can help other teens discover who they are and where to go next.

4

DOLLARS AND SENSE

There are some things you need to know that you didn't even think you needed to know. Even though money management is a daily part of our lives, young adults like yourself aren't always fully prepared for what lies ahead. That's why there's a whole chapter dedicated to this topic.

The bottom line is that your future depends on your ability to not only make money, but to spend it—wisely.

As a young adult, you may not be too concerned about taking control of your finances, but the earlier you start, the better off you will be when you reach retirement. When you learn to budget and manage your money in other ways, you can rest assured that you'll have the finances to cover living expenses such as rent and food when you stop working.

I know that you may not be extremely excited by the prospect of spending your money wisely and saving what you can. You have this newfound freedom and the last thing you want to do is spoil it in any way. Don't worry, I'm not going to ask you to implement unreasonable financial rules.

Learning about money isn't all about becoming rich. That may be one of your goals, but there's more to being money savvy. Managing money is good for

- understanding the value of money
- growing your savings
- creating and sticking to budgets
- letting your money work for you

Ultimately, knowing how to handle money makes you a more responsible adult.

MONEY MANAGEMENT TIPS

To help you take control of your finances, here are some top tips for young adults.

Take Charge of Your Own Future

There are different routes you can take when you learn how to manage your finances and there will be just as many opinions. Your dad may tell you to buy real estate, while your uncle may think putting your money in stocks is the way to go. Although you should appreciate their advice, there's no one who knows your finances better than you do.

Don't do something just because someone tells you to. Do your own investigation and take charge of your future. Read books, go see a financial advisor, and after you've done all you can, manage your money in a way that suits your financial situation.

Track Your Spending

At the end of the month, do a recon of how you spent your money. When you know exactly where your money is going, you'll be able to make changes based on your end goal. You may see that your morning coffee and bagel at the corner coffee shop are impacting your budget more than you thought. Just changing this one habit can have a huge impact on your finances.

It's not about cutting out all your guilty pleasures, it's about making sure you're sticking to your budget to avoid any unwelcome surprises as month-end nears.

Set Goals

In Chapter 4, we established that setting goals is an important aspect of living a fulfilled life. Financial goals are no exception.

If you don't plan ahead—in other words, set goals—you will end up living from paycheck to paycheck, and that is not truly living.

Buying a car or house, getting married, going on vacation, traveling, and so on are all mini goals you need to work toward. Saving enough to retire comfortably should be your main goal.

Instead of spending your money on worthless items, think big. If you don't, and you just recklessly buy what you want at any given moment, you may regret it later. One way to guard against frivolous spending that will distract you from your goal is to work a spending allowance into your budget.

The 50/30/20 Rule

In the previous point, we touched on spending wisely so that you can meet your goals. There is one specific budgeting system that works great to align your saving goals with your spending. Known as the 50/30/20 rule, it comes down to separating your after-tax income into three categories: essentials, wants, and savings.

Essentials will make up most of your budget at 50%. This includes paying rent, buying food, and any other vital expenses and financial responsibilities you have. Thirty percent goes toward treating yourself. You can use it for that daily bagel and coffee you had to give up, to buy clothes or anything else that isn't strictly necessary. The last 20% goes into your savings account.

I have to mention that the above order isn't the way you should approach this money management plan. First, take care of the essentials, then save, and when you've done that, you can spend. You should always meet your responsibilities first before spending money, and seeing saving as a responsibility, will lead to financial success.

Plan for Emergencies

Good financial management includes having extra money stashed away for emergencies. It doesn't matter what your salary is, you need to put some money away for a rainy day. A good rule of thumb is to save up at least three to six months' worth of income. This emergency cash will give you peace of mind. Saving for emergencies should be non-negotiable.

Negotiate Your Salary

You have two options when it comes to saving. You can either lower your expenses or negotiate for a higher salary. Spending less is much less intimidating than approaching your manager for an increase. However, if you can build the courage to ask for more money, you won't have to sacrifice the things you love, but you will improve your financial status.

The worst thing that could happen is them denying your request. On the flip side, if they say yes, your life will change for the better.

Save for Your Retirement

I've emphasized the importance of saving for retirement, but a further tip I can give you is that you shouldn't wait to start—the earlier you put money away for when you're ready to stop working, the better off you'll be.

Retirement plans are based on compound interest, which isn't the easiest of things to understand, but the basic principle is, the sooner you start, the less you'll need to save to reach the amount you need to retire comfortably. In other words, if you save $100 a month now, it will be more valuable than saving $1,000 a month later in life.

Companies usually offer retirement plans, which is a great way to get started. You'll be investing pre-tax dollars into an account and the company will match your contribution.

File Your Taxes

You don't want the tax man to come knocking at your door. I know doing your taxes can be intimidating, but it is one of those things you have to do. The good news is there are not only people who can help you, but there are also software programs that make the process less painless.

Even if doing your taxes is a bore and you feel it is such a "grown-up" thing to do, remember, you have new responsibilities that come with your recent independence. There's another positive to filing your taxes: getting money back. There are deductions that can put money back in your pocket, so before you file, make sure you do some research on what you can claim.

Look After Your Credit Record

Your credit score can open and close many doors for you as an adult. If you have a positive credit history, you can get a credit card, qualify for a loan to buy a car or a house, etc. Considering the importance of your credit score, you need to make sure you pay your bills on time. A good debt-to-asset ratio is also imperative if you want to make credit work for you.

When you do get a credit card, be wise. It's easy to go overboard with spending with a credit card—swiping a card and not affecting the money in your account immediately takes away the need to stick to your budget. The problem is, the next month, you're going to have to pay it back and you'll definitely feel your previous splurge then.

Make Money

Unfortunately, your generation will have to work harder to save enough money for retirement. Working a 9–5 may have been enough for your parents and their parents, but you won't necessarily have that luxury. Freelancing and entrepreneurship are growing trends because you have more control over your financial future that way—you know if you work hard, you'll make more money. What's even better about this new trend is that you can create multiple revenue streams; you may have a normal 9–5 job but supplement your income with a freelance job on the side.

Depending on the career you choose and the growth possibilities in your job, you may have to do something extra to boost your income.

Money shouldn't be your enemy. However, if you don't make it work for you, you will struggle with finances throughout your life and when it's time for you to retire, you may not have enough saved up to do so comfortably. The best advice I can give you is to make money your friend by following the tips above.

This chapter is short and sweet because, although money management can be complicated when it comes to investments and stocks, it is simple in all other aspects. The main thing you have to remember is to spend wisely and save what you can monthly.

KEY TAKEAWAYS

- Money management is important if you want to reach your goals.
- You're going at it alone now and that means you have more responsibilities, and making sound financial decisions is one of them.
- Don't spend impulsively. Create a budget and stick to it.
- The 50/30/20 rule is a beginner-friendly way to start managing your finances.
- Most importantly: Save, save, save.

5

LET'S GET PERSONAL

Your relationships with friends and family aren't exempt from the changes you're going through as you move to adulthood. The dynamics will start to shift as you grow older and become wiser; some relationships will end, while others will grow stronger. The world of romance is also opening up more, and your intimacy with others doesn't have to take place in secret anymore.

All in all, the transformation you're going through has some pros and cons when it comes to the relationship department. In this chapter, I'm going to give you the knowledge you need to navigate the subtleties of relationships as a young adult.

We'll also take a look at romance and sex, and what you can expect.

Strap in; we're going to cover some personal stuff in this chapter!

FAMILY AND FRIENDS

Your family can be an invaluable support system. They're usually there to celebrate with you when you succeed but won't shy away from giving you comfort when you're going through a difficult time. That doesn't mean it's sunshine and roses all of the time. Family fights, misunderstandings, and disagreements are a reality, but if you're lucky, they're minor enough to resolve on their own through some clear communication. However, toxic family dynamics cannot be ignored, and in these instances, conflict can ruin relationships.

If you're part of an unstable family dynamic, you have to realize that it can affect your health and well-being in the long run.

- You may blame yourself for growing apart.
- Family or holiday events may be a major source of anxiety.
- You may withdraw from your family, which can make you feel like you don't belong anywhere.
- You may find it extra difficult to get through emotionally or financially difficult periods as there's no support from your family.

Luckily, you're old enough to take steps to minimize the effects that family tension has on your health. There are some things you can do to attempt to repair family bonds. Let's look at the most common reasons why family relationships are on the rocky side, and what you can do to smooth things over.

Finances

You're leaving home, but that doesn't mean your parents will stop wanting to control your finances. This is particularly true when they're paying for college. They may have strong opinions on how you spend your money and that can be a source of frustration for you. You're growing more independent and likely don't want anyone to treat you like a teenager. Siblings may also compare how much money each gets from their parents, and if there is a difference, it may cause a fight.

The best way to overcome these types of money-related problems is to:

- **Be selective with what you share:** You don't have to share your financial status or spending habits with your parents or your siblings. However, if your parents are paying your college fees and also ensuring that you have a roof over your head, it's best to not waste their money. They most probably worked very hard to save enough to make sure you get a higher education; don't disrespect them by blowing it on parties and frivolous purchases.
- **Set boundaries:** Don't be afraid to tell your parents or siblings when they've crossed a line. When your family members want to dictate your finances, and you've given them no reason to question your money-management skills, then let them know you won't tolerate their behavior.

Growing Family

As your family grows, so does the possibility of conflict. When you meet a girl or boy and decide to marry them, it changes the structure of your established family and opens the door for tension. The well-known trope of the evil mother-in-law is an example of just how complicated things can get.

To get along better with new and extended family members:

- **Respect the differences:** Each family unit is different. Your family may be super into spending holidays like Thanksgiving together, while others may be more relaxed and go with the flow. Culture and environment impact behavior and tradition and that can cause problems if not respected.
- **Focus on the positive:** Your brother-in-law, stepmother, or other new additions to your family are there because they're valued by someone else. There is good in each of us and focusing on the positive traits of others will go a long way in keeping harmony in the family. When you find yourself annoyed with something a family member is doing, remind yourself of one of their positive attributes instead.
- **Find common ground:** It's not often that you come across someone you share no interests with. Ask about their hobbies and passions and you may just come across something relatable that will strengthen the bond between you and any new family members. If you can't find any commonalities, remember that the

biggest link between the two of you is that you both love the same person in some capacity or another.

Unresolved Issues

The past can have a profound effect on the present. I'm not necessarily talking about holding grudges, although that does play a part in how people treat each other. Unresolved family drama can also have a lasting impact on relationships. If you and your mother had an argument where hurtful things were said and the issue never got resolved, it may be difficult to move on and make your relationship grow.

The bad thing about issues that haven't been dealt with completely is that they tend to creep up on you. You may think everything is fine and the altercation is forgotten until it raises its ugly head at a family event, celebration, or during times of change. You need to fix what needs to be fixed, and this is how you can do it:

- **Speak up:** If you're the one who can't let go of what happened in the past, let the other person know. They may be in the dark as to why you're giving them the cold shoulder, so give them the chance to repair the relationship by telling them what is wrong. You don't have to be confrontational; share your perspective in a kind and loving manner and give them the chance to apologize if they want to.
- **Have empathy:** If a family member resents you for something you did in the past, don't become aggressive when they try to tell you about it. Offer them the same

courtesy you'd expect if the roles were reversed. Listen to what they have to say and if your past actions hurt them, apologize, but don't stop there. Ask them what else you can do to repair the relationship.

Interacting With Difficult Family Members

Let's face it, some family members are nearly impossible to get along with for whatever reason. Although you may want to avoid them altogether, that won't always be possible during weddings, funerals, and other family gatherings.

If you can't avoid having contact with a difficult family member, here are some other things you can do to make sure you make it through the day:

- **De-Stress Beforehand**

You know there's a family event coming up and you're dreading it. Instead of wallowing about how much you don't want to go, start doing some stress management techniques to prepare you for the day. Meditate, take daily walks, journal your thoughts and feelings, or spend some time with a close friend; whatever you choose to do, it should be relaxing.

When you're at the event itself and you start feeling anxious, take a moment to ground yourself. Excuse yourself from the room and look for ways to clear your head. You can breathe in and out a few times, visualize something relaxing, or find a dog or cat to pet. This should make the stress melt away, which means you'll be able to tolerate your family member again.

- **Stick to Your Boundaries**

Boundaries are so underrated, and if you do happen to believe in them, you may get villainized by others for saying "No" so easily. You shouldn't care about losing popularity points because you have limits. When you have to go to family get-togethers, boundaries can protect your mental health. For example, if there is a specific topic that is a no-go zone for you, you can let your family members know and if they continue to talk about it, you can get up and leave. If they get angry with you for leaving, it's on them because they crossed the line.

The only thing you have to remember is to stay civil. Don't get angry at anyone if they cross your boundaries. You want to be clear about what your limits are, as well as what the consequences will be if they're crossed. Do keep in mind that no matter how respectful you are in communicating your boundaries, there is a high likelihood that people will still be offended. Having personal limits is a foreign concept to many. You'll also get people who believe in setting boundaries for themselves, but don't respect the boundaries of others. Ultimately, it's not about protecting someone else's feelings; it is about taking care of yourself.

Some examples of areas where you can set boundaries are:

- **Borrowing and using your things:** There are some things just too valuable to us to allow others to borrow them. You're allowed to say "No" when asked if they can use it.

- **Your time:** I'm a big proponent of me-time. You need to take time for yourself to recharge your batteries. If you're invited to go out and you really don't feel like it and would much rather stay home and watch a movie, that's okay.
- **Your privacy:** Family and friends should respect that you don't want to share everything with them. Some things are too personal to share with even the closest people in your life. You need to figure out where to draw the line for prying family and friends.

Those are only three examples of where you may want to set boundaries; there are many more. You can also have separate boundaries for friends, family, and work. If you're still wondering how to go about setting limits, here are three tips to get you started.

1. Figure Out What You're Willing to Tolerate

You can't set boundaries if you don't know what you are and aren't okay with. Your values and priorities are good guides as to what your boundaries should be. Alternatively, you can simplify things and look at what makes you feel good and what doesn't, and work from there.

2. Let Others Know What Your Limits Are

When you know what your boundaries are you can tell others. It's only fair that others know what you will and won't tolerate. I know this process isn't easy because you don't know how someone will react, but if you respectfully share your limits, while considering their feelings, you've done all you can. After you've communicated your boundaries, you have to make sure that you consistently enforce your personal limits—if you don't, people may think you're not serious about them.

3. Learn to Say "No"

For a very short word, it sure has a lot of power. Saying "No" enforces your boundaries. Of course, actually uttering the word is difficult if you're used to letting people walk all over you. If you suddenly assert your limits, people may get offended and may even feel hurt. That is a reality of living with boundaries, but they have to understand that you're a person too, and what you want matters. How you say "No" also impacts the other person's reaction. You don't have to sound aggressive or offensive—assertive is the vibe you should go for.

Work on Your Emotional Intelligence

To manage your emotions, you need to have high emotional intelligence (EQ). What's more, high EQ also helps you identify and cope with the emotions of others. This will have a positive effect on family relationships and will protect you from unnecessary confrontation.

If you want to enhance your EQ, you first need to work on self-awareness. To lay a strong foundation of EQ, you should:

Examine yourself: Every person has a role to play in a family system. Often, we hold our family responsible for some of the issues we have to deal with today. That isn't only unfair, but it is a fallacy. You need to take accountability for your own health and happiness. If it happens that your family truly did hurt you in some way, it's your choice if you want to keep a grudge or work toward forgiving them. Once you attend to your own emotional health and stop playing the victim role in your family, many of the problems you may currently have with family members will get better.

Stay consistent: You can't be emotionally aware today but tomorrow have the EQ of a banana. When you're not consistent, your loved ones will get confused and maybe even frightened. Work on staying aware of your feelings, thoughts, and behavior when you're around family members to ensure that you don't act out of character and break the trust of your loved ones.

Be careful of destructive memories: You'll always be your parents' child but as you grow up, your role will shift slightly; you'll be less afraid to let them know when you don't agree with them. However, when you get triggered by a negative emotional memory, you may find yourself reduced to a six-year-old who is being scolded for stealing a cookie. If you don't have emotional intelligence, you may feel out of control when this happens. It is best to take some time to reflect on which memories are so strong that they can reduce you to a child again.

Don't limit yourself to the past: To some family members, you'll always be the little brother or sister, or the sibling who skipped class to spend the day playing Xbox. It can be infuriating if you've grown to be more than that and have accomplished things you'd rather be known for. If this is something that bothers you, use your EQ to change the narrative. For example, when you see your family, don't travel back in time and discuss the past; instead, focus on what is going on now. Afford your family members the same courtesy of not limiting them to the past.

Focus on the Good

Even difficult family members have some positive attributes. I know it is much easier to focus on their shortcomings, because who wants to look for the good in someone who is known as being a problematic link in the family chain? However, if you want to keep the peace at family events, don't stare yourself blind at their flaws—if you look hard enough, you'll notice their strengths.

Show Compassion

Stop to consider if your family member is going through a hard time and that is why they're being less than pleasant. Maybe they're facing financial problems, have personal insecurities you don't know about, or are struggling with mental illness. There are many underlying factors that can contribute to their behavior. I'm not saying their circumstances should excuse their behavior, but maybe if you take a more compassionate approach, you'll be more understanding when you're finding it difficult to be around them.

Limit Expectations

You're not going to like everyone—even if they are family. You're also not going to agree with all your family members' viewpoints, priorities, or behavior. That is okay. If you accept this, you'll be able to manage your expectations and appreciate the relationship for what it is.

Make and Keep Friends

I have good news: Making friends is much easier when you're not in high school. The social maze you have to navigate as an adult trying to make friends is much less complicated. Yes, you still have various peer groups you have to find your place in, but rejection isn't as devastating as it was in school because your self-worth is (hopefully) starting to improve.

That being said, the social and emotional wounds you may have suffered during school can leave lasting scars that can impact you well into adulthood. For example, if you were a social outcast, you're behind when it comes to developing social skills, which will make it challenging for you to start and maintain friendships.

If you were an outsider throughout school, don't worry, you can learn the lost skills you need to become more social as a young adult.

The problem is that romantic relationships always steal the spotlight, and there isn't much guidance when it comes to fostering friendships. This is surprising since good friends are there for the highs and lows of our lives, while boyfriends or girlfriends come and go. We often also have stronger bonds with our friends than with family members because we spend so much time together.

Considering this, it is understandable how true friendship, or the lack thereof, determines our level of happiness. So, it's not a matter of *wanting to* develop long-lasting friendships that can grow into the tightest of bonds; it's a matter of *having to*.

Here are some tips for making and keeping friends:

1. It's About Quality, not Quantity

Saying you have 700 Facebook friends doesn't hold much meaning. Do they actually know the true you and not the social-media version of you? Have you gone for coffee with all 700 of them recently? The fact is, these relationships are pretty hollow, and what's worse, they can actually make us feel lonelier than if we had fewer friends on social media (Ali, 2018). Despite this, we continue to scroll through a sea of strangers we call friends, and attempt to build relationships with thumbs up, heart, and laughing emojis. The sad part is that these superficial friendships take time away from forming relationships with substance. Stop fooling yourself; instead, spend time creating a handful of friendships that are real.

2. Think Of It as a Matter of Health

Social support plays an important role in your health—mental and physical. No, really. One study found that not having social relationships increases your mortality rate the same as smoking 15 cigarettes a day does (House et al., 1988). That's beyond crazy! Supportive friendships also lower your stress levels

(Ozbay et al., 2007). As you become an adult and face new challenges, you need all the stress-busters you can get.

3. Don't Give Up Too Easily

Although making friends is somewhat easier as you age, you don't have the benefit of the close proximity to people as you do in high school, except if you go to college. This just means you need to work a little harder to be part of groups where you can make friends. You can go to art classes, join a book or movie club, or do something else that involves socializing. If your social skills are what they should be, you'll make friends in no time. However, if you're somewhat of an introvert, you'll have to work on overcoming the anxiety that usually goes with meeting new people.

I also don't want you to give up if you fail at making friends. This can be especially hard if you weren't the popular kid in high school. Just remember that it has nothing to do with you. Life happens and the timing may not be "just right" for the other person.

4. Show You're Interested

Small talk is tedious, but it's often the first step to getting to know someone. You shouldn't fall back on it, however. You should find a way to dig deeper so that the person sees you are interested in them beyond their job and the weather. Pay attention to everything they say; they will drop a hint that you'll be able to ask them about at a later stage. Also, don't hold back in sharing something personal about you. If you show them that you feel safe being vulnerable around them, they'll open up more. This is the only way you can transition from talking about small stuff to building a deep friendship that will last for ages.

5. Keep the Momentum Going

Life happens and people get busy. You may call a friend and they are too busy to answer. Then when they return your call, you're the busy one. It's easy to feel like you don't really matter to them, which makes it appealing to just give up. Don't! Work around busy schedules by setting a time to meet up—decide on a time that suits both of you and stick to it. Your weekly or monthly meet-up will soon become a habit and your relationship will grow.

6. End Toxic Friendships

You may be afraid to end friendships because you have too few friends, or you keep thinking of all the time you put into building a relationship with someone. However, don't force it. Some friendships aren't meant to last. In fact, a friendship should end when it causes you stress and affects your self-esteem or well-being negatively. If you dread spending time with that person, you should take that as a sign that this friendship isn't meant to be. Don't let familiarity and guilt drive you to keeping unhealthy friendships going. To help you spot toxic people in your life so that you can avoid adding them to your close friend circle, here are some signs you should look out for:

- They're overly critical and judgmental.
- You feel happy when you go to see them but walk out feeling horrible about yourself.
- You have to constantly explain yourself and defend your decisions to them.
- You dread seeing them.
- They manipulate you for their own benefit.

Friendships are about giving, but you should also get something in return. If you're not working toward a common goal of growing and nurturing your relationship as equals, then they're not true friends. Toxic people like manipulating others. Don't fall victim to it.

ROMANTIC RELATIONSHIPS

Forming and maintaining a romantic relationship is a milestone of becoming a young adult. Erik Erikson, a well-known developmental psychologist, described this time in your life as "finding oneself yet losing oneself to another" (Cherry, 2022). That just underpins the importance of romantic connections in young adulthood.

However, before you can experience intimacy with someone, you need to know yourself enough to be able to commit to a long and meaningful relationship. You need to know what your values and needs are because intimacy is often based on commonalities in these areas.

But how do you go from friends to partners? What exactly do you need to do?

From Strangers to Romantic Partners

Research done in 1973 shows that starting a relationship has six stages or tasks to complete (Davis, 1973). This is interesting, considering that we experience our interactions with each other as unique. Now, you may be thinking, that's a very old study that can't still be relevant today. Well, rest assured, the findings of this study are still widely used in relationship counseling and therapy in general.

Let's explore Davis's six steps to starting a relationship.

Step 1: Ask yourself, "Does this person qualify?"

You have to evaluate whether a person is worth your effort. Are they kind, intelligent, funny, or good-looking?—these are only some of the aspects of attractiveness.

Step 2: Find out if your romantic interest is available.

Look for a wedding ring or someone who is more than a friend by their side. There's no use in pursuing someone who is already taken.

Step 3: Do something to grab their attention.

You may decide to use a pick-up line, or maybe you're more of a "strike up a natural conversation" kind of person. There's not really a right and a wrong here. The main aim is to see if they're still interested in talking to you after your first interaction.

Step 4: Keep their attention.

When you have their attention, it's now up to you to keep it. To do this, Davis (1973) recommends using a topic that entertains both of you. The more you share interests, the bigger the possibility of stumbling onto similarities, and that is fertile ground for attraction to blossom.

Step 5: Represent yourself.

Remember, it's not only you who's sussing out the other person. With this in mind, present a version of you that you think they will be attracted to. A lot of people will say, "Just be yourself," and that is true in some regard, but there's nothing wrong with highlighting some aspects of yourself that will increase your chances of forming a romantic relationship.

Step 6: Plan the next encounter.

You have to make sure that your first conversation is not the last conversation. You need to mention that you're keen on a subsequent get-together.

Did you instinctively follow the steps above with your high school sweetheart or did you skip one or two? Or maybe you're now scratching your head because your advances failed even though you did everything you just read?

The process of starting a relationship is very fragile, and sometimes, despite your best effort, it fizzles out before it even starts. It's a good idea to look at why that happens so that you don't get discouraged when not all your romantic interests return the sentiment.

Why Do Some Relationships Not Work?

There are many variables that impact successfully starting a relationship. For example, the person you're interested in may already be in a relationship, or maybe they're not giving you the attention you desire, which impacts their attractiveness. You also have to consider that they don't want anything serious right now because they're going through a stressful time or are preoccupied with studies or finding a job.

Take time to look at your role in someone's indifference. It's anything but easy to keep an intelligent conversation going while you're trying to portray yourself as an appealing party and you're drowning in nervousness. That's a lot to juggle, and sometimes you just can't keep all the balls in the air.

Other times, the location and atmosphere throw a spinner into the works. For example, you may be in a club where the music is too loud, and they can't hear your quirky replies. Or maybe your friends keep interrupting the conversation. You may spot a boy or a girl that piques your interest but there just isn't an opportunity to strike up a conversation. You win some and you lose some. I always tell my kids, "If it is meant to be, it will be." So, don't get too upset if you spot someone and the conditions aren't right to express your interest. Maybe you'll see them around again! If not, then someone better may be waiting around the corner.

Sex

I wouldn't be surprised if exploring your sexuality is high on your to-do list as a young adult. It may be a new experience for you and you can't wait to experience the physical and emotional pleasure that comes with having intercourse. Even if you were sexually active during high school, your curiosity about sex isn't likely to change for a while yet.

There aren't many decisions you'll make in your life that are bigger than the choice to be sexually active before marriage or to wait until the big day. There are many opinions and varied beliefs on the subject. This is a decision only you can make. We have talked about quite a few things to help you get to know yourself better—you have the tools to discover your core values and principles—and I hope it will help make this decision a little easier for you.

Take your time and really think about this decision. Being sexually active is a ton of responsibility and if you consider the things that can go wrong (unwanted pregnancy and sexually transmitted infections [STIs]) the emotional turmoil of making the wrong decision can be devastating. It's a serious decision with serious consequences.

Since sex requires serious consideration, I'm going to ask you some questions you need to answer before you take the final leap and have sex.

Questions: Personal Values

What are your inner feelings about having a sexual relationship at this moment?

Be honest with yourself. Do you think it is appropriate behavior for your age? Is it something you really want to do, or are you considering it out of peer pressure? Does it feel like the right thing to do in your heart and mind? It's your body, so don't let anyone pressure you into doing something you don't want to.

What do your parents and religious leaders think about having sex at your age? Do you agree with them?

You didn't grow up in a bubble; your parents' moral and religious beliefs were part of your upbringing. Your cultural tradition and religious heritage may be very important to you and going against what you've been taught to believe can cause many negative feelings. For this reason, consider your upbringing carefully before you make a final decision.

How will you feel if others (including your parents) know that you're having sex?

We're told not to judge others for their actions, but unfortunately, some people do. That is something you need to consider. You'll need to decide if you can live with their feelings about what you're doing. Then there are your parents. How will they feel about you having a physical relationship with someone? But more importantly, how do you feel about their thoughts on the matter?

Do you accept the risks that go hand-in-hand with having sex?

Although having sex can be an intimate and fun activity, many people feel that a person needs to be more emotionally mature to handle the potential consequences. As a young adult, many may argue that you don't yet have the emotional skills to navigate any emotional, physical, or health issues that may arise from being sexually active. If you become pregnant or catch an infection, a few minutes of pleasure will leave you with long-term consequences that could affect any future relationship. You have to weigh up the positives and negatives and make an informed decision—don't just focus on your desire for sexual gratification.

Questions: Relationship

Do you trust the person you're considering having sex with, and do you feel safe with them?

If you're feeling awkward, nervous, or unsure about who you want to have sex with, then they're not the one. Feeling safe during sex is an absolute must, and you shouldn't settle for anything less.

Can you discuss the topic openly and honestly with your partner? Have you?

A lot of questions need to be answered truthfully before you go ahead. If they get angry when you ask them about previous sexual encounters and if they've ever had or currently have an STI, then you should see red flags. You also need to find out what their thoughts are about using contraceptives. When yours and their views don't align, then they're not a sexual match for you. If you haven't had such a candid discussion with them, then now is the time. And if you have the conversation with the attitude of keeping their wellbeing in mind too, they're more likely to be open to the conversation.

Why do you want to have sex with this specific person?

Sometimes, there's a negative reason behind the desire to be intimate. Maybe you're in a relationship where they've given you an ultimatum: either have sex or they're leaving. Maybe you think they'll love you more if you agree to sleep with them, or perhaps you want to do it because all your friends are. Those are all unhealthy reasons. If your answer is not, "Because I've taken my time to consider it, and, I feel good about taking this step," then I recommend you wait a little longer.

Questions: Practical Matters

Did you pay attention in sex ed class?

Do you understand how women get pregnant? What are the common STIs you should be careful of contracting and what are their symptoms? Where do you get condoms? What other methods of contraceptives are there? These are all questions you need to know the answers to or you're not ready to have sex.

What is the course of action if someone gets pregnant? What do you do if you or your partner gets an STI? Who would you turn to if this happened?

Contraception is not foolproof, and sometimes unplanned and unwanted things can happen. Think about what you'll do if it happens. What would your parents do? Will you have the resources to manage the situation? I don't want to be a Negative Nelly, but it's best to be prepared for the worst-case scenario or you'll be even more overwhelmed.

Having Sex for the First Time

Deciding to have sex is not to be taken lightly. When caught in the moment, your hormones and emotions may get the best of you if you haven't taken the time to answer the above questions. Talk to your boyfriend, girlfriend, or alternatively, a trusted adult, and make sure you're emotionally and physically ready. More importantly, have sex because you want to, not because you feel pressured.

What will happen to my body?

There are no outward signs that will make people say, "Ah, they had sex!" During the act, however, you may experience some changes to your breathing; it can become heavy and intense. Your skin may become flushed, and you may start to sweat. Your body will return back to normal after sex.

Will it be painful?

Women may experience some pain on penetration as their hymen stretches or tears. There may be some bleeding but that isn't always the case. For the most part, there will be some discomfort and not intense pain. There's also a chance that the hymen was broken before sex through activities like horse riding, for example.

You may also experience some sensitivity due to friction during penetrative sex. To prevent this, you should ensure there is enough lubrication to facilitate entry of the penis into the vagina. Foreplay stimulates natural vaginal lubrication, but there's nothing wrong with applying extra lubricant to make sex more enjoyable.

Can I get pregnant?

Yes. It's as simple as that. If you don't wear a condom or you're not on some form of birth control, the chance that you'll get pregnant does exist. I know there are some people who believe that it's not possible to conceive your first time having sex, but the fact of the matter is, if you've started menstruating, you can get pregnant. I also have to mention that using the pull-out method, where the man removes his penis from the vagina right before orgasm, doesn't work, and can lead to pregnancy.

Will I have an orgasm?

You may have this idea that your first time is going to be magical and everything is going to be great. The truth is that your first time will most likely not be as perfect as you imagine. The nervousness both of you are feeling, as well as the mild discomfort you may experience doing the act itself, may lessen your chances of having an orgasm. On the other hand, if you're a man, you may be so excited that you won't last long and it may be over before your partner has had time to orgasm. That's perfectly normal and you shouldn't feel embarrassed. Sex without orgasm can still be fun and it can help you explore other ways to reach that "wow" moment.

Safety First

You should be aware of ways to protect yourself and your partner from unwanted pregnancy and infections. Safety should always be at the forefront of your mind, even though it may be difficult in the heat of the moment. Be prepared and carry condoms with you for the eventuality that you'll be intimate.

STIs

If you don't use protection, your risk of contracting chlamydia, hepatitis B and C, syphilis, genital herpes, gonorrhea, and HIV/AIDS increases significantly. It's true that some of these diseases will go away after a course of antibiotics, but some are incurable and come with severe health implications. Considering the seriousness of STIs, always have a chat with your potential sexual partner about their sexual history and their willingness to practice safe sex.

Contraception

Barrier methods that stop sperm from reaching the egg are one of the most popular methods of contraception. If you're a woman, you may want to consider going on some form of birth control like the pill, patch, or implant called an IUD. These all affect your hormones by stopping an egg from being released. Of course, these protect you from unwanted pregnancy but do nothing to stop STIs. No protection method is 100% effective, so doubling up is not a bad idea.

Feeling confused is common—having sex for the first time is a foreign experience. You may also experience some anxiety, but if you're with the right person in the right place, and practice safe sex, you'll feel more comfortable and can enjoy the experience.

EFFECTIVE COMMUNICATION

I'm ending this chapter with a section on communication because if you can't converse with someone, you're not going to have much success in the relationship department.

When I talk about effective communication, I don't just mean sharing information. There's more to it than that. To be a good communicator you need to understand the intention behind the information you're sharing and the emotions it will stir up.

Communicating with someone, especially a stranger or romantic interest, can be nerve-wracking. You know what you want to say, but the words come out of your mouth all muddled. Add to that, the possibility of your already garbled message being lost in translation and you have a recipe for disaster.

Effective communication does not happen instinctively; many people have to actively work at improving this skill. If you want to work on your communication, you may want to think of what barriers are holding you back in the first place.

Communication Hurdles

There are some common obstacles that stop us from being effective communicators. If you can identify these, you can eliminate them one by one until you reach your full potential in the communication department.

Overwhelming emotions: It's not possible to have a conversation if your emotions are all over the place. Neither you nor the person you're talking to will benefit from a conversation driven by out-of-control emotions. If you can't calm down, the chances of your chat leading to conflict and misunderstanding increases.

Multitasking: If you want to be an effective communicator, you need to put down your phone, stop daydreaming, and prevent yourself from planning what your response will be. Multitasking and effective communication don't go together. Not only is it disrespectful, but it will also make the person you're talking to feel unimportant.

Contradicting body language: The words that you speak must correspond with your body language. For example, saying "No" but nodding your head in agreement is extremely confusing. Worse yet, if your words and body language don't match up, the person you're talking to may think you're busy lying.

Negative body language: We're going to have a closer look at nonverbal communication in the next section, but crossing your arms, tapping your feet, and avoiding eye contact are all forms of negative body language that send the wrong signals. Even if you don't agree with what is being said, you should make certain that your body language doesn't come across as aggressive or uninterested.

Nonverbal Communication

Your body has a language of its own, and you'll be surprised to hear that this is actually our primary way of communicating. Yes, we may exchange dialogue, but our body speaks much louder and is often way more honest.

Our facial expressions, eye contact, tone of voice, how we sit or stand, and posture all communicate nonverbally. If you understand body language, then it will be so much easier for you to connect with others and build relationships. Nonverbal communication is often more honest, as it happens unconsciously, and is harder to manipulate than words. So, you'll be able to read clues as to how a person is really feeling and then you can adapt your communication strategy accordingly. Even when someone is silent, they're still communicating nonverbally.

All this counts in your favor as you can use your knowledge of body language to be more sensitive to the thoughts and feelings of others, which will definitely score you brownie points with your family, friends, and romantic partner.

Of course, it's not all about reading others' body language; you also need to be aware of what messages you're sending.

Facial expressions: Your face is extremely expressive. You don't need to say a word, just by looking at your face, it will be possible to tell what you're feeling. What's interesting is that, while other forms of nonverbal communication are influenced by a person's culture, facial expressions are universal. Sadness, happiness, fear, anger, and more are expressed nonverbally, in the same way, worldwide.

Posture: Have you ever judged someone based on how they stand, sit, walk, or place their shoulders? You're not the only one. How you carry yourself communicates a lot about who you are. For example, if your shoulders are slumped forward, people are going to read that you're insecure and lazy. So, be mindful of your posture, stance, and the subtle movements you make while verbally communicating with someone.

Touch: A firm handshake, a congratulatory pat on the back, a loving hug, or a patronizing tap on the head all have a message. Make sure you're not crossing a communication boundary by using the wrong type of touch in a specific situation. For example, if you're trying to impress someone, you're not going to grab their arm in a controlling way. This will tell them that you're forceful and aggressive, which will make them bolt in fear.

Voice: Your tone of voice is important as it can indicate affection, confidence, anger, and so on. How fast or slow you speak also influences how others receive your message.

Space: "Respect my bubble," is something I taught my children from a very young age. Personal space is sacred to many, and if you invade it, you may be conveying a message of aggression and dominance. Of course, if it is your girlfriend or boyfriend, getting into their bubble can communicate affection and intimacy. It all depends on the person and the situation. Also, keep in mind that the size of personal space very much depends on the person and their culture. Some cultures will be okay with you getting up close, while others will want you at arm's length or more.

To be successful at forming and maintaining relationships, clear communication is key. I hope this chapter showed you just how important it is to have a social support system, and what you can do to keep your relationship with family, friends, and partners healthy.

In the next chapter, we're facing some demons that you hopefully won't have to battle—but if you do, I want you to be as prepared as possible.

KEY TAKEAWAYS

- Being part of an unhealthy family dynamic can affect your physical and emotional health.
- Finances and unresolved issues from the past are two of the main reasons for discord in families.
- There are things you can do to make spending time with difficult family members more bearable. Setting boundaries and working on your emotional intelligence are only two examples.
- Having close friendships increases your happiness, but remember, they need to be quality friends, not superficial social media friends.
- Getting involved in a long-term relationship is a milestone of young adulthood.

- There are six steps to starting a relationship that guarantees success, but sometimes, outside factors interfere.
- There are many things you need to consider when having sex for the first time.
- When you decide to be intimate with someone, do it because you want to, and not because you feel pressured to.
- Always have safe sex. Unwanted pregnancy or getting infected with an STI can have long-term effects.
- Effective communication can make or break relationships.
- Your body says a lot more than you think, so make sure the words coming out of your mouth correspond with your nonverbal communication, or people will think you're not trustworthy.

6

FACING THE HARD STUFF

As if what we've covered thus far isn't difficult enough, we're now going to delve into some extra-intense topics. We have to because substance abuse, drug addiction, and mental illness are harsh realities for many.

SUBSTANCE ABUSE AND ADDICTION

A person is considered addicted to something when they compulsively and repeatedly use alcohol, drugs, or other substances despite the negative impact it has on their lives—physically, mentally, and socially. When you're addicted, you often experience physical and psychological dependence on the substance, and when you don't have access to it, you experience withdrawal symptoms. Depending on the drug of choice, these withdrawal symptoms can range from mild to deadly.

Even though addiction is a hot topic, the problem isn't getting better. Between 15 and 29 million people are addicted to a variety of substances, including alcohol (United Nations Office on Drugs and Crime, 2017).

In the US alone, there are thousands of drug and alcohol rehab centers, but still, the problem persists.

The best chance we have at fighting addiction is to educate people—when we understand what addiction is, and how it functions, we can fight it. Addiction is stubborn and it traps a person in their situation. If people don't understand that, it's quite likely that treatment will fail.

The three main factors that make addiction so insidious are cravings, depression, and guilt. If you, or someone you know, want to get clean and stay that way, all three of those factors must be dealt with.

Rehabilitation centers usually use medicine to curb cravings during recovery, which opens the way to deal with the more mental aspects of addiction, namely depression, and guilt.

Depression

When someone is trying to get sober, the depression is usually so heavy that it drives them back to using. This is why it is important to keep an eye on a person's mental state, and help them overcome their depression, if you want them to stay clean long term.

The depression that accompanies getting sober is caused by physical and psychological factors.

Physically, their body's natural chemistry is wrecked. Some drugs are powerful stimulants that make the body run at 100 mph, while other drugs slow down these functions. Alcohol does both. You can see how a drug addict or alcoholic's body isn't running how it should. This imbalance of chemicals includes the happy hormones serotonin, dopamine, and norepinephrine. The result? Depression.

The psychological reasons that cause depression are obvious in the case of someone battling addiction. They feel worthless, like failures, and they can't see their life ever improving. Their thoughts are negative, constantly focusing on their predicament. They usually also don't live in the best circumstances, which only makes matters worse. In other words, their inner bully is taking advantage of their addiction to ramp up the criticism, the scathing comments, and self-deprecation.

Guilt

No one wakes up one day and decides to become an addict. Often, a person's first drug experience happens in a social setting. Peer pressure can play a role in accepting a joint or a pill, or maybe the fact that other people do it, and seem to be okay, puts a person more at ease. Before you know it, drug use becomes more frequent—instead of doing it with friends at a party, you may decide to smoke some marijuana daily to relax. And don't think you're immune to it because you live in the perfect home and family environment. You're not!

It's a slippery slope between using drugs recreationally and becoming addicted. What's worse is, often when the excitement or effects of a milder drug fades, people move to heavier, more dangerous drugs.

Before you realize you have a problem, you're blowing your monthly budget on more drugs. To help you pay your bills, you may start to borrow money from loved ones—all the time knowing that you won't pay them back. You may even steal from family members to get enough money for your next fix.

When it comes to your job, the effects of the drugs may lead to you making unnecessary mistakes, taking too many sick days, and behaving badly in the workplace. It's highly likely that you'll lose your job. This puts you in more of a financial dilemma and so things spiral out of control until you're living under a bridge and have nothing left. It happens. Often!

It would be hard for anyone to live with themselves after doing the dishonest, damaging things that drug addicts are known for. The only time you will be able to escape the guilt is when you're high, which means you'll want to be high more often to escape the guilt, and you become trapped in a vicious circle of addiction.

Thankfully, it's possible to rid yourself of the guilt by beating your addiction, asking for forgiveness from those you've harmed, and most importantly, forgiving yourself.

Causes of Addiction

Why did you get addicted in the first place? As I mentioned, no one wants to become a slave to anything, so why then does it happen? Well, there aren't any conclusive answers and there's still much to be discovered. What we do know, is that there are four main factors that play a role:

1. **Psychological**: People with mental health issues or significant emotional distress are more prone to substance abuse, as they use drugs or alcohol to escape from their minds and numb emotions that overwhelm them.
2. **Biological**: If there's a history of substance abuse in your family, you have to be careful, as you're more vulnerable to addiction.
3. **Environmental**: The cards you've been dealt aren't always good, and some people have an especially bad hand. If you suffered parental neglect, you may drink or take drugs to get your parents' attention, or if you grew up in a house where doing drugs was the norm, then you may not know better.
4. **Physiological**: If you've been using drugs for a long time, your body undergoes physiological changes that will leave you physically dependent on the substance. In other words, if you stop taking it, the pain and other physical discomfort will drive you back to doing drugs.

It's usually not any one of these factors that lead to addiction, but a combination of them. For example, if you're genetically predisposed to addiction, and you grow up in an abusive household where drugs are used openly, these factors together, can lead to drug abuse.

Recovery

I know it's hard to talk about substance abuse, partly due to the guilt you may be feeling. However, talking to your parents or another trusted adult is the first step to getting the help you need. There are many support groups and resources available to addicts; you just need to reach out and ask for help.

If you're totally opposed to talking to someone you know, look for a recovering adult support group online. Have a chat with people who've been where you are and have overcome their addiction. You don't have to face this problem alone.

MENTAL HEALTH

You're going through a time of change and, as we know, change usually comes with a good dose of stress. When you experience prolonged stress, as you'll be doing while you transition to living independently, you're more vulnerable to mental health issues.

In fact, young adults face more mental health issues than seniors aged 65 years and older (Sapien Labs, 2020). That's not only concerning but, also saddening. Young adults are in the prime of their lives; they shouldn't be struggling with such heavy emotions.

So, why do young adults have such a negative outlook on life? Let's look at the most common reasons why life may look somewhat overcast:

Lack of sleep: Let's face it, your schedule has filled up significantly since you've stepped into young adult life. If you're studying further, your academic workload just adds to an already long list of things to juggle. When you're not studying, you may be working or socializing with family or friends. This means getting a full eight hours of zzz's doesn't happen often, and when you don't get enough sleep, your mood will be affected, which will impact your outlook on life.

Massive change: We've talked about all the changes you're going through extensively throughout this book. This also means you'll have to make a lot of big decisions. What career path you want to take. If you want to further your education, and in what direction. Where you're going to live, and with whom. And, whether or not you're ready to get into a serious relationship. These are only some of the things you'll need to consider. This can cause a lot of stress.

Uncertainty: We're living in uncertain times. Your generation has witnessed many scary and significant events: terrorist attacks, school shootings, and the first global pandemic in decades, to name only a few. What's next? The uncertainty that comes with the future is a major source of stress, which can trigger anxiety disorder, as well as depression.

Brain development: Your brain is still growing and, despite this, you have to make hard decisions. Basically, you're making life-changing choices while your brain is not running at its full capacity. Your prefrontal cortex, which is the decision-making part of your brain, still has some developing to do. Again, the worry, second-guessing, and possible guilt that this causes, opens you up to mental health issues.

Your mental state may be somewhat fragile right now as you enter young adulthood, but there are ways you can become more mentally resilient. Practicing gratitude, self-care, mindfulness, and many other things we covered in this book, will make you strong enough to reach adulthood with flying colors.

The most important thing is that you stay alive. If depression pulls you down into a very dark and lonely hole where you see no light, please reach out. When you take your life, you may believe you're putting an end to all your troubles, but you're also taking away your opportunity to live, laugh, and love. There's always a way out; you just need to ask someone to show you. I once received some valuable insight; "One thing in life which is guaranteed is "Change". When you know this upfront, you know what to expect, and change won't seem like the world is out to test your resolve. You'll be ready to "roll with the punches", so to speak.

KEY TAKEAWAYS

- Substance abuse and drug addiction are an unfortunate fact of life.
- You're addicted when you don't worry about the physical, mental, and social impact your drug or alcohol use has on your life.

- To fight addiction, people need to understand that there are three factors to treat if they want long-term results: cravings, depression, and guilt.
- Drugs take a toll on your physical well-being. They cause a chemical imbalance, affecting your happy hormones, and this is why you get depressed when you're addicted to a substance.
- Someone who is addicted to drugs has a negative outlook on life. They don't see a way out and end up feeling like failures. This opens the door to depression.
- You may find it difficult to live with yourself considering all the bad things you may have done to get your hands on drugs or alcohol, but that guilt can be overcome.
- Young adults are more prone to mental illness because of the changes they're going through and the big decisions they have to make.

And remember, when you anticipate change in your life, you'll be more flexible and ready to deal with it.

WHO DO YOU TURN TO FOR ADVICE?

Teens rarely listen to adults and we get that! However, it's normal for you to relate to and understand where other young adults are coming from. This is why your opinion matters so much.

There is a teenager out there rolling their eyes at their parents but on the inside, they really need some help!

A massive thank you for your time because I really do get that you are busy. Make sure you let me know how you are getting on in your review. I love to hear from you because your generation is the future!

CONCLUSION

Congratulations! You survived all those years living with your parents, although you didn't think you would, right? I know, parents can be such buzzkills at times. But, here you are, ready to venture out into the great big world.

There's no denying that being an adult is hard, but being a young adult is even harder. You've been taken care of all your life and now suddenly you need to take care of yourself. Making friends was easy—well, as easy as it gets in high school —but now you'll have to find other ways to meet people and form friendships. Did I mention that romantic relationships now include the possibility of sex, marriage, and children? The list of changes you're facing is long, but so is the list of opportunities.

You're going to start a career, build meaningful relationships, and will be able to buy a car, a house, or rent a fancy apartment. These are exciting times, and I hope after reading *Adulting Life*

Skills for Young Adults, you feel a little more prepared—more at ease.

I'm proud of you. The fact that you took the time to read this book shows that you care about your future. That you want to make a success of the one chance you get on planet Earth. That is a promising sign that you're going to put in the work needed to not only find your purpose, but to live it!

You've learned how to live life on your own terms, true to your core values and beliefs. You're not going to let anyone, not even you yourself, bully you into believing you can't make your dreams come true.

All you need to do is adapt to the changes happening in your life, but if you keep an open mind and don't fall into a rigid thinking pattern, transitioning from a teenager to a young adult should be a breeze. Oh, and don't forget to apply creative thinking to your life. The decisions you make will be more in line with your core values if you think outside the box.

As you enter this new phase of your life, remember to set goals. Your aspirations and dreams are destinations on a map that brings you to your ultimate goal: living a long, happy, and authentic life. Healthy habits will keep your body and mind strong as you move through life, smashing one goal after the other. So, make eating well, drinking enough water, exercising, reading, and traveling part of your daily routine.

Thank you for trusting me to guide you through this important step in your life. I hope you walk away feeling prepared and excited about what lies ahead. But before I leave you to go lead an independent life, I want to impart one last piece of wisdom: love. Love deeply and wildly and continuously! Not just your friends, family, and partner, but life itself.

If you value what you read in this book and feel that it helped you, please give it a favorable review. Better yet, tell other young adults about it, so that they can start their journey, with this book as a guide.

REFERENCES

Ali, S. (2018). Is social media making you lonely? Psychology Today. https://www.psychologytoday.com/us/blog/modern-mentality/201810/is-social-media-making-you-lonely

Cherry, K. (2022). Erikson's stages of development: A closer look at the eight psychological stages. Verywell mind. https://www.verywellmind.com/erik-eriksons-stages-of-psychosocial-development-2795740

Davis, M. (1973). Intimate relations. New York, NY: Free press.

De Bono, E. (2016). Six thinking hats [Book]. Penguin Life.https://www.amazon.co.uk/Six-Thinking-Hats-Edward-Bono/dp/0241257530/ref=pd_bxgy_14_img_2?_encoding=UTF8&psc=1&refRID=1TQP079QQHRWTF07MAF3

DeBruhl, R. (2023). Your 10-step guide to modern car care. AARP. https://www.aarp.org/auto/car-maintenance-safety/modern-car-care/

Ghosh, P. (n.d.). Low self-esteem 'shrinks' brain. BBC Science. http://news.bbc.co.uk/2/hi/health/3224674.stm

Goliszek, A. (2014). The stress-sex connection. Psychology Today. https://www.psychologytoday.com/us/blog/how-the-mind-heals-the-body/201412/the-stress-sex-connection

Goodreads. (n.d). Benjamin Franklin: Quotable quotes. https://www.goodreads.com/quotes/460142-if-you-fail-to-plan-you-are-planning-to-fail

Hendriksen, E. (2016). How not to care what other people think. Scientific American. https://www.scientificamerican.com/article/how-not-to-care-what-other-people-think/

House, J.S., Landis, K.R. & Umberson, D. (1988). Social relationships and health. Science, New Series, 241:4865, 540-545. https://www.jstor.org/stable/1701736

Internet Encyclopedia of Philosophy. (n.d.). https://iep.utm.edu/ethics-and-contrastivism/

Ozbay, F., Johnson, D.C., Dimoulas, E., Morgan, C.A., Charney, D. & Southwick, S. Social support and resilience to stress: From neurobiology to clinical practice. Psychiatry (Edgmont), 4(5):35-40. https://www.ncbi.nlm.nih.gov/pmc/articles/PMC2921311/

Locke, E. A., & Latham, G. P. (1990). A theory of goal setting & task performance. Prentice-Hall, Inc. https://psycnet.apa.org/record/1990-97846-000

Pew Research Centre. (2012). Young, underemployed, and Optimistic. https://www.pewresearch.org/social-trends/2012/02/09/young-underemployed-and-optimistic/

Ryan, T.A. (1970). Intentional behavior: An approach to human motivation. New York: Ronald, 14(1), 575 pp. https://doi.org/10.1177/000276427001400111

Sapien Labs. (2020). The mental state of the world report. https://mentalstateoftheworld.report/

Schwartz, S. H. (1992). Universals in the content and structure of values: Theory and empirical tests in 20 Countries. In M. Zanna (Ed.), Advances in Experimental Social Psychology (Vol. 25, pp. 1-65). New York: Academic Press.

United Nations Office of Drugs and Crime. (2017). World drug report. https://www.unodc.org/wdr2017/index.html

Velasquez, M., Andre, C., Shanks, T. & Meyer, M.J. Ethics and virtue. Markkula Centre for Applied Ethics: Santa Clara University. https://www.scu.edu/ethics/ethics-resources/ethical-decision-making/ethics-and-virtue/#:

Weghofer, A., Himaya, E., Kushnir, V.A., Sohat-Tal, A., Barad, D.H. & Gleicher, N. (2013). Is immune system activation/systemic inflammation a prerequisite for successful reproduction? Fertility and Sterility, 100(3):S329. https://doi.org/10.1016/j.fertnstert.2013.07.956

Made in the USA
Monee, IL
14 August 2024

fb1b9fd6-4812-42b0-9200-7550c484ab8eR01